Zen Shin Talks

by
Sensei Ogui

Compiled and Edited
by Mary K. Gove

ISBN 0-9658352-1-9

Cover and chapter page design: Ihor Gernaga
Japanese calligraphy: Koshin Ogui
English calligraphy: Garth Proctor

Published by: Zen Shin Buddhist Publications
P.O. Box 181134
Cleveland, Ohio 44118-1134
e-mail: marygove1@juno.com

Library of Congress Cataloging—in Publication Data
Ogui, Koshin. 1940-
    Zen Shin Talks by Sensei Ogui,
Compiled and edited by Mary Gove, 1945-
p. cm.
ISBN 0-9658352-1-9

We are grateful to Sue Nelson for reflecting on and giving feedback in shaping Sensei's Dharma Talks into this book, to Kristi Rowe for interviewing Sensei, to Carolyn Ahern, Jim Redford, Jerry Pevahouse, and Andrea Tiktin for tirelessly proofing the text, to Thomas Salomon for making Zen Shin Talks visually beautiful, to Jessica Gove for her patience with her mother, and for the Reverend Kono Scholarship Fund for making the publishing of this book possible.

Contents

Foreword

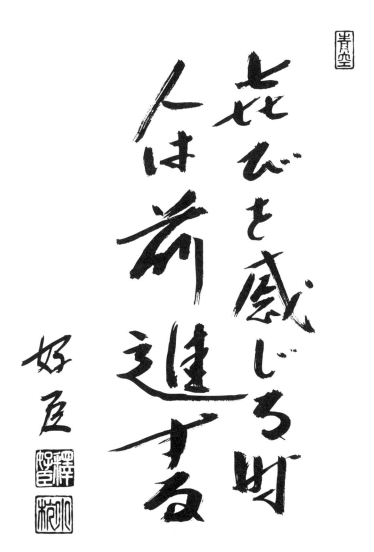

喜びを感じる時
人は前進する

好互

"When we enjoy,
one's life goes forward"

Someone wrote a book called *How the Swans Came to the Lake*.   In the book Buddhist teachers, mainly from the East, are regarded as *swans* and the United States is considered as the *lake*. It is a well-written book.

Those who appeared in the book are one of the flock of *swans* that flew to this *lake* before 1960 following Japanese immigrants. One of the outstanding *swans* in the flock, is Sensei Koshin Ogui. He not only flew in but made this *lake* for both Americans and Japanese. He merged the Pure Land School of Buddhism with Zen Buddhism creating Zen Shin Sangha. This creation required confidence and courage, as he had to overcome sectarianism. Sensei Ogui did this historical task in the most natural way.   His warm openhearted personality attracted numerous individuals: religious people with differing backgrounds, people in business, doctors, artists, and those from many other fields.

During   the sixties when Americans were attracted to Buddhism, people wondered why.   In the seventies, when Americans were attracted to Buddhism, people started to understand and countless Centers or Sangha, were born on the *lake*. Now at the end of the twentieth century the Buddhist population in the United States is innumerable.   It was an inevitable phenomenon, whether Americans are aware of it or not. Living in the midst of capitalism and Puritanism, it was necessary for them to find that, "This very Body is the Body of the Buddha."

This book, by Sensei Koshin Ogui, opens a new perspective to Americans. This did not come out of his knowledge, but his wisdom, compassion and profound understanding of human weakness, as well as strength, grief, and joy. He went through all of these. That is why this book penetrates into readers' hearts.

Eido T. Shimano
Abbot of Dai Bosatsu Zendo
Catskill Mountains, New York
September 1, 1997

Preface

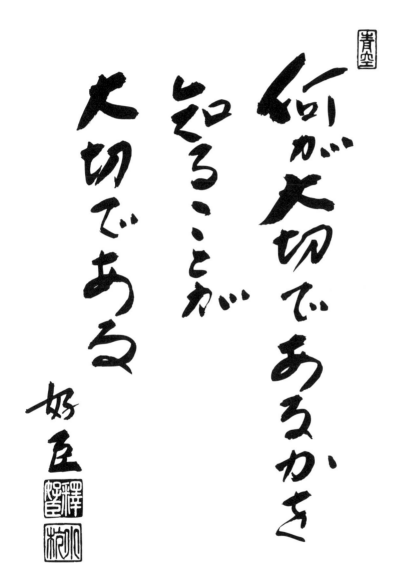

"To know what is an important matter
is important"

To know what is an important matter
is important.

This is the message in Sensei Ogui's calligraphy on the preceding page. Having known Sensei for the last 15 years has been important for me. Having his thoughts and ideas available to people in a book *is* important.

Zen Shin Talks by Sensei Ogui is about spiritual practice in America today. Sensei Ogui teaches a down-to-earth form of Zen and Shin Buddhism. He is quite engaging and humorous. Many of his Dharma Talks are in response to the energy of those sitting in front of him listening. Sometimes he engages the listeners in short conversations. In these talks Sensei Ogui recounts stories and personal experiences with compassion and humor. He illustrates the way we human beings often disregard the aliveness of each moment and expresses with exceptional insight the Buddhist perspective on every day life.

Zen Shin Talks by Sensei Ogui is for people who want to explore their spirituality more deeply. *When you walk in the rain you get wet*, says Sensei. This is true be you Buddhist, Christian, Moslem, Jewish, male, female, Black, White, Japanese, German, a mother, a dentist or whatever.

In 1983 a friend brought me to the Cleveland Buddhist Temple. I listened, then, for the first time to Sensei's words. Afterward, his words returned to my mind as I proceeded through my hectic day-to-day life. One of the first phrases which came into my mind again and again was, "You are the only one with your life." This had an important psychological effect of on me. I began looking more carefully at what I was doing with the moments that made up my life. I noticed that his words, when focused on with sincerity, had a calming affect on me and helped me grow spiritually.

One of Sensei's messages is to ask ourselves *What can I learn from this experience?* Through thinking of each and every experience in this way, we can change the quality of our lives. I found that through thinking in this way, I was able to move away from victim thoughts such as *John is so mean, Harriet hurt me, Bob did this and that to me.* But there is more to his message. *Watch your mind. This is a way to take care of yourself and practice effortless kindness to others.* Also, *See the humor in what happens.* "I laugh at myself a lot," says Sensei Ogui.

We each think similar ideas as "the Bible says . . ." or "a great Buddhist teacher says . . ." I realized such thoughts are not important. What is important is how much we are aware of the changing nature of our being, that we are each *changing, becoming and moving on* as Sensei Ogui would say.

Many of the illustrations used in Sensei's talks come from his own life. At times he attempts to use words to explain the undescribable. At other times Sensei Ogui tells stories or uses koans to help those listening grasp a certain awareness and thus grow spiritually. Koans are puzzles which can't be solved intellectually, but rather must be applied uniquely in each one's daily life.

Day-to-day interactions are another way of teaching for Sensei Ogui. In this way he changes the lives of many of those he meets. Herbert A. Selwyn, a realtor in the Cleveland area who was told by his doctor he had only a few months to live, spoke of his friendship with Sensei Ogui:

I met Reverend Ogui while playing golf. We were introduced and paired up by a golf course employee whose duties entailed keeping play on the course moving smoothly. How fortunate for me! From this accidental meeting, an extremely close personal friendship resulted. I've taken a great deal from this relationship. Spending time with Reverend Ogui was always enjoyable and frequently educational. My life changed. Through his influence I am better able to accept life and deal with the undesirable consequences. Sensei Ogui has afforded me the opportunity to live my life not knowing the answers. The ability to deal with "what is" has helped me endure the less than positive happenings which visit me. A major positive change in my philosophy of life occurred, even through my negative experiences. This treasure, for it *is* truly a treasure, is available to all who choose to accept his lessons.

Sensei would say that this meeting with Herbert Selwyn, as well as Herbert Selwyn's physical condition, were both a manifestation of *things as they are*, the universal truth of the Dharma. A person who has an awareness of universal truth may think *So it is.*

Zen Shin Talks by Sensei Ogui was written over an eight year span of time. In putting Sensei Ogui's Dharma Talks onto paper, I made an effort to retain his sense of rhythm and thought, but found it necessary to edit out some of his idiosyncratic language patterns. Seigen Yamaoka, former Bishop of the Buddhist Churches of America, read a review copy of *Zen Shin Talks* by Sensei Ogui and wrote, "As I read his words, I could feel his presence. I was amazed that you were able to capture his presence... It's really great. Namu Amida Butsu."

Several of my friends helped me with the editing of *Zen Shin Talks*. Three of them claimed the Buddhist label and two did not. All of them remarked that they needed time to reflect on his thoughts. One friend said she had a disagreement with her husband. They read part of the text to each other, and this helped them resolve their differences.

Thus, I recommend you read *Zen Shin Talks* slowly. Please read one talk, savor the meaning, think about how it speaks directly to your life. Share this with a friend. Your friend does not need to know about Buddha Dharma. Rather try to communicate the message that Sensei is trying to communicate. Hold this awareness in your mind throughout the day and see what comes into your mind. If it appeals to you, keep a journal of your thoughts.

This book grew out of the enthusiasm of those who listened to Sensei Ogui's Dharma Talks and wanted to read and to preserve what he teaches. So please enjoy *Zen Shin Talks* as much as I have!

Mary K. Gove

About Sensei Ogui:

Sensei Koshin Ogui is an eighteenth generation priest of the Japanese Pure Land Sect of Buddhism, also referred to as Shin Buddhism. He has extensive training in both Zen and Shin practices. Sensei Ogui's Zen training includes experiences in numerous institutions in Japan and with Suzuki Roshi of the San Francisco Zen Center, author of the popular *Zen Mind, Beginner's Mind.* In addition, Sensei Ogui has studied world religions at Yale Divinity School. Sensei Ogui is a registered minister with the Buddhist Churches of America with headquarters in San Francisco. A trustee of the Parliament of World Religions, he works to build up understanding among people of different religions so that they will appreciate each others' traditions and uniqueness. Sensei Ogui is often requested as a speaker by religious groups throughout the country. Currently he resides in Chicago with his wife, Mayumi, and his step daughter, Ayaka. He is resident minister of the Midwest Buddhist Temple and overseer of the Cleveland Buddhist Temple. Sensei is an avid golfer and a master calligrapher.

About Mary K. Gove:

Mary K. Gove PhD has been listening to Sensei Ogui's talks since 1983. She is Head Senior Leader of Cleveland Zen Shin Sangha, an organization founded by Sensei Ogui. She has recently retired as a Reading/Writing educator where she worked in an inner city urban school district. She is co-author of the best selling educational methods text *Reading and Learning to Read,* published by Harper Collins. She is also an education professor at Cleveland State University. Mary finds time to be actively involved in spiritual growth groups. She is a member of the Circle of Directors of Among the Pines whose dream it is to create a holistic center for the integration of body, mind and spirit in Northeastern Ohio. Mary lives in Cleveland with her daughter, Jessica. She practices yoga as well as Zen and loves to swim laps in community pools and to spend time with her friends.

A Note:

Sensei Ogui and Mary Gove plan to write a second book with more of Sensei Ogui's Dharma Talks, as well as written experiences and insights of people who hear Buddhist messages and apply them to their life. If you have such experiences and insights, please send them to Mary Gove, Cleveland Buddhist Temple, 1573 East 214th Street, Euclid, Ohio, 44117 , or e-mail marygove1@juno.com for possible inclusion in this second book. Thank you.

One

Am I taking care of my life?

" It exists, only one life to live"

*Things are not what they seem; nor
are they otherwise. Realize it. Make
it yours. Repeat this puzzling phrase
over and over, endlessly. Then the
impact will come through in your
daily experiences. The truth is always
manifested by itself in our life.*

THINGS ARE NOT WHAT THEY SEEM;
NOR ARE THEY OTHERWISE

I was flying on a plane. As the plane neared San Francisco, both the young couple seated next to me and I looked out the window and saw a beautiful scene -- crystal blue water, sea gulls swooping gracefully in a cloudless sky, tiny white triangles of sail boats dotting the seascape, vivid green hills in the distance and a bridge with sunlight reflecting from it.

The young couple exclaimed to each other, "Look at that! The Golden Gate bridge! It looks like a post card. Splendid!"

I thought to myself, "This couple is so enthusiastic! They express their feelings so freely. Truly beautiful!" I then noticed that the bridge in our view was not the Golden Gate Bridge, as the couple thought, but the Bay Bridge. I wondered, "Should I tell them?"

I said, "It doesn't matter what you call the bridge, but that is the Bay Bridge, not the Golden Gate Bridge. Soon the Golden Gate Bridge will come into view."

In a few moments a second bridge, the Golden Gate Bridge, came into view. It too reflected the sun with the picture post card scenery surrounding it. At this moment a memory had an impact on me. I flashed back in time to when I was a minister in the San Francisco Bay area. I was in the coroner's office and

I heard the voice of a mother as she identified the body of her twenty-year-old daughter who had flung herself off the Golden Gate Bridge.

I heard this mother scream with a voice which seemed to come from hell, "What a chicken! What a coward! How dare they not understand my sadness and grief. I'd like to die too, but I can't because I have three living children to take care of."

This mother spoke with enormous energy. Such grief this mother felt!

I recalled my involvement with this family. First, I had talked with the father who had asked me what to do about a twenty-year-old daughter who had committed suicide in Japan. I had told him to bring the ashes of his daughter back from Japan. When he did so, I conducted a memorial service for the family and friends at the temple.

Two weeks after the memorial service, a young man met with me because his father had committed suicide by jumping from a window onto concrete pavement. As I wrote down the death record, I noticed the address was the same as the one for the twenty-year-old suicide victim. I inquired and was told this man who had committed suicide was the father of this twenty year old girl. So there had been two suicide deaths in this family.

I visited the family three times and I noticed a twenty-two-year old daughter was acting very strangely. I told the mother this daughter needed professional help. The mother responded and the daughter was hospitalized. The daughter recovered rapidly and was allowed to visit her family. After her visit, she returned to the hospital, organized her possessions there, and called a taxi to take her to the Golden Gate Bridge. There she flung herself off the bridge to her death.

Often bodies of suicide victims who take their lives by jumping into the bay from the Golden Gate Bridge are not found. But in this case, the daughter's body was found. I had gone with the mother to identify the body. So the almost unearthly sound of the mother's voice came back to my mind as I looked out the window at the Golden Gate Bridge from which the girl had flung herself. The sound of her voice was in great contrast to the voices of the couple next to me who were exclaiming, "Beautiful! Splendid! Like a post card!"

I was quiet as we gazed at the same bridge which brought to mind the anguished cry of the mother when recognizing the body of her daughter. I wondered, "Is it nothing but *splendid, beautiful* as this couple exclaims? Or is it *treacherous, miserable* as the anguished mother exclaims?" After a short pause, I realized that the Golden Gate Bridge *is as it is* -- the boats, the sea gulls, the hills in the distance, they are as they truly are -- at this moment so calm, so peaceful.

Then another impact came to my mind. These are not the same sea gulls that the couple and I see as the ones which were circling the bridge when the girl jumped from the bridge. The bridge seems the same, but it does not remain the same over time. With this realization and awareness, I talked to the young couple. They shared with me that they were on a honeymoon to San Francisco. I agreed with them, "The Golden Gate Bridge is beautiful, gorgeous, impressive and magnificent enough to be put on a post card."

The Golden Gate Bridge evoked powerful emotions from the mother whose daughters and husband had committed suicide and from this couple sharing the view for the first time as they honeymooned. Our Western-trained minds think of these strong emotions as negative and positive, miserable and elated. But our truthful mind sees that the Golden Gate Bridge with the surrounding scenery is as it is. It *is* beautiful. Also it *is* changing. Even within a few minutes the sea gulls and sailboats are in different places. Billowing clouds moved into our view as the plane flew lower preparing to land. You may think, "But the bridge is static. It doesn't move. It doesn't change." But the bridge, too, is changing. It is moved by powerful winds. Its metal beams are slowly eroded by wind and rain. In order to slow down this erosion, the bridge is constantly being painted. Workmen start at one end of the bridge, taking a year to paint the entire bridge from one end to the other, only to begin again.

Things are not what they seem; nor are they otherwise. Realize it. Make it yours. Don't waste your time and energy. Your daily experiences are very important. View them as your practice or *shugyo*. *Shugyo* literally means to accomplish your life. Do not ignore whatever happens in your life. Each of us has life circumstances. Each of our lives is different. But one aspect of life which is true for each of us is that our life circumstances are changing. Nothing is the same day to day, even moment to moment. Does this sound scary? Do you wonder, "How can I control these changing circumstances?" You can't. Don't even try.

You may ask, "How can I take care of my life?" Don't worry that such and such will happen. Don't create such anxieties. Rather, wait and see what happens, wait and see what events occur in your life. Feel anguished or elated if such feelings are part of the experience. That's part of being human. But don't categorize life experiences as negative or positive, miserable or happy. Then whatever happens, let it happen.

Think, "How can I take care of it? What can I do to learn from it?" Instead of being caught by a happening, rather see it, face it, overcome it and learn from it. This is the attitude of someone seeking the meaning of life.

A Buddhist monk and his student were walking on a forest path together on a beautiful spring day. As they turned a corner they heard a flapping sound. They had startled a wild goose which rapidly flew away. The teacher said to the student, "What is this?"

The student said, "A wild goose flew away in the eastern direction."

Then the teacher grabbed his student's nose and twisted it.

The student didn't understand. He said, "Why did you do that?"

The teacher just smiled.

As a clue to help you become aware of what this story can mean in your life, I say, "What you think is what you get."

SEPARATION FROM YOUR TRUE SELF

Most Zen teachers would tell the story above and then stop talking. In American culture, though, I have to talk; I have to explain. Sometimes, when it comes to expressing genuine feelings, just holding hands or giving someone a hug are ways we express deep feelings of love and caring. No words are needed. But in the case of a Zen story like this one in this culture, words may be needed.

After I told this story I'm sure many of you were thinking, "This story doesn't make sense. I am confused." This is a helpful way to be because then this story may remain in your consciousness.

Since this story does not make sense in our normal way of thinking, it may seem hard to learn from this story. We have been habituated with a certain way of learning from nursery school up through college and into our adult working lives. In contrast, a Zen Buddhist teacher wants to give an impact which brings about a different way of learning. This way of learning is different from blindly believing what a sutra or a Buddhist textbook says. Rather the Buddhist challenge is to learn through experiencing. Bang! Ask yourself, "What am I aware of in my life due to this teaching?" This is the way of fresh wisdom, not knowledge. With our practice we want to break through simply acquiring knowledge; we want to break though preconceived ideas of trying to fix something. Then a new vision or way of living our lives will be born.

So it is my karma to be here to talk about this different way of learning and to explain this story to you. The teacher intentionally asked the student, "What is it?" This question seems to be a common ordinary question, but to the teacher this question was a test of the student's awareness. The student said, "The goose flew away in an eastern direction." The Zen teacher didn't say anything. He just twisted the student's nose.

If this happened in our American culture, a Zen student may ask the teacher, "What did that mean?" The teacher might respond, "Might I say something to show you what this meant?"

You could say, "The forest is beautiful this spring day, isn't it?" This response shows the student has an awareness of being in the forest *right now*. Instead of this kind of dialogue so familiar in our culture, the Zen teacher twisted his student's nose without saying any words. This teacher was actually being patient instead of talking to the student. The student's nose ached after being twisted. The teacher twisted his student's nose to let him know *You are here. You shouldn't fly away.* Most of the time as we are seeing, saying, and doing, we are separated from *I am.* The teacher was teaching the student not to lose one's true self.

So now after this explanation, what can you do so you are not separated from your true self? Practice your answer in your daily life.

I took some lessons from a professional golf instructor once. He showed me how to grip the golf club. He said I should grip the club as if I were holding a bird in my hand. He said, "If you hold the bird too tight, it will kill the bird. If you hold it too loose, the bird will fly away."

We usually think that we should hold something we prize tightly and hard, and we feel assured that by holding it tightly, we have strength or power over it. But this is not true. When we tighten our grip over a golf club or a prized possession, our movements become tight so that we lose coordination and timing.

The grip you use in golf is important -- not too tight, but not too loose. The same principle applies to relationships. Yes, in relationships, in a sense, we do have a possession, but why not possess it softly? Work to create mutual understanding. Work to keep up respect with each other.

GOLF AND BUDDHISM

When I was taking lessons from a professional golf instructor, he taught me about taking a proper stance before I swing my club. He told me to stand with equal weight on both feet, to direct the alignment of my feet to the spot where I want to drive the ball. He said my feet are to be parallel to each other like a "train track", with this "train track" pointing directly toward my target. According to Jack Nicklaus, you can't hit the ball straight to the flag if your stance is not pointing that way too. When someone points out that my stance does not point toward the flag on the green, I get irritated. I think, "Don't talk. I need to concentrate."

Often I think that my stance is straight. One day I was taking my stance to hit the ball, when one of my friends humbly said, "Hold it." He placed his golf club in line between my left toe and my right toe and asked me to step back to see the line of my stance. I could not believe it! Instead of my stance pointing directly to the flag on the green, it was pointed to the side. I was very grateful to my friend for so clearly showing me that my stance was crooked when I thought it was straight.

Most of the time, I'd say ninety percent of the time, I think my stance is straight and aligned with my target, but when I check, it is not really in line. We think we are straight and aligned, but it is not really so. We think we understand, but it is not really so.

You are listening to my talk right now. If I asked each of you to write down what you heard, each would describe my talk in a different way. It's amazing and beautiful how each of you would uniquely write down different things. This same phenomenon would occur if five children from the same family were asked to write down what their father had told them. Each one, even from the same family, will uniquely understand the words they hear from someone else.

We listen, yet we are not fully listening. We all have preconceived notions. Usually we say something is "good" because it agrees with our preconceived ideas or ideas we already have. We all have been nourished with different ideas as we are brought up and these often stay with us. These are the ideas to which we often say, "That is good." So when we hear a speaker who fulfills our expectations, the words he says satisfy us. But such a speaker only reinforces what we already knew and believed. We have not learned anything in this case. For different people the same speaker will have a different impact. So what you learn is your responsibility, not the speaker's responsibility. This is why it is so difficult to really learn and integrate teachings into our daily lives, to experience enlightenment.

When I am sure that my golf stance is straight, that's when I need to truly listen to others. When you think, "I am very sure," it is very likely that you are misleading yourself. Shakyamuni Buddha clearly awakened to the fact that one of the main causes of human suffering is that we cannot see things as they truly are. We see things through our convenience and judge them from there. It is hard to realize our wrong views.

It's nice to have a good friend and teachings which direct me to the right views. *The worst enemy in our life is to believe that "I'm absolutely right."*

One way of transcending knowledge and making it wisdom used in our daily life is through working on koans. Koans are sayings which are enigmas, that is they don't seem to make much sense. Koans are frequently used in Zen practice. For example, one koan is *Things are not what they seem; nor are they otherwise.*

When I ask Zen students what such a koan means to them, I get very uniquely different responses. The impact is different for each one. We are each very unique, and this uniqueness is very respected. Why not be unique and the best of your uniqueness? From this point you may find a way to live your life.

So I have a firm but gentle grip on my club; I have listened to my golf partner, even when I was *sure* I had a straight stance.

Now it is time to hit the ball. My golf instructor tells me to hit through the ball, not hit the ball. When I think about hitting the ball, I am very attached to the ball. This is especially true when a fellow golf player has just hit a long shot. I'd like to hit farther than he did! I try to think about what my golf instructor has told me, what I have read, what I have heard from others. And all these *are* important. But trying to recall what I have been taught, throws off my coordination between my mind and body. Thus, I should not leave what I have been taught as sayings and feelings. I need to make these things a part of my life. I need to forget about these ideas, to simply play, to simply live.

What does the Middle Path have to do with my life?
My father gave me a fan. On one side of the fan it reads in Japanese, "If I don't do it, who will?" On the other side it reads, "If you did not exist, the world would not change much."

THE MIDDLE PATH

One hot summer day I was in my office, soon to officiate at a funeral service. The Assistant Minister was working hard preparing the temple for the funeral. As I sat in front of my desk, I thought, "What should I talk about at the funeral service?" I was in a quandary. When we visit friends who have lost their loved one, we often cannot find adequate words. We are usually quiet. We can shake their hands or hold them as they cry. That's the best way. Just be there. But as the minister, I am obligated to talk at the service. That's a minister's karma.

Sometimes we as human beings realize that the death of a loved one does not mean to be totally sad every moment. An extreme case which illustrates this is a person who has been bedridden for years and finally dies. Even in this instance, we would not say, "Hey, congratulations! Your father finally died." Instead we compromise and look for some reasonable words to say like, "It is a blessing that he died." Also we may think, but not say in public, such things as, "Hey, I heard your father left a million dollars in life insurance." Likewise, we would not say out loud when a spouse died, "Now, you have a chance to find another mate." These thoughts streamed through my head as I was trying to concentrate on what to say at the funeral. As a minister, these thoughts seemed complicated and difficult to me. What should I talk about?

I felt hot, so I began fanning myself. I continued thinking. I thought that it is easier for Christian clergymen and clergymen of other religions which emphasize faith in one God. The Christian minister can comfort people at a funeral by saying, "Your loved one is in God's hands." However, in the Buddhist approach, we must nourish wisdom. As a Buddhist minister I try to encourage awareness in the people. A Buddhist minister needs to give some kind of impact. "Hey!" I was thinking and thinking. My ego rose. I thought, "I will say something good, so the audience will tell me, *Your talk was brilliant!*" In this way my ego cheered me up.

It was hot. I continued to fan myself. I innocently looked at the fan and noticed that on one side of the fan was written in Japanese, "If I don't do it, who will?" This refers to you doing what needs to be done. Then I looked at the other side of the fan. It said, "If you did not exist, the world does not change much." These two sayings are quite opposite, aren't they? I thought, "What it this?" These words were written on the fan by my father who passed away quite some years ago. As I sat in my office I thought, "If you don't do it, who will?" Yes, indeed. I also thought, "If you did not exist, the world does not change much." It is true.

We think a big part of our lives is our relationship with our mate. Yes, our mates do make a big difference in our lives. But if your mate dies, your life *will* go on. There is always a chance you will find another mate. Also, mothers, as they think about their children, feel a great need to make sure their children are fed, clothed, and educated. Mothers think, "How will my children be able to grow up without me?" Yes, it is true; as a mother or a father, you do much for your children. You do

many things to support them as they grow up. Yet, if you died
or disappeared, someone would take care of your children. But
don't say, "Who cares? Someone else will take care of my
children." This attitude would lead you to neglect your children.
This is an extreme attitude to be avoided. On the other hand, to
think, "No one else can do this," is also extremely one-sided.

I thought, "I am the one to conduct this funeral service."
On the other hand, I thought, "If I have a heart attack and die
right now, the assistant minister will take over. Or someone else
will take care of it." Yes, that's right. I felt confused. How
could both be true?

Then I noticed the gentle breeze from the fan coming
through and cooling me off. Both sides are unified, blended.
Both sides melt into the cool wind. This is how the middle path
guides me to harmonize my life.

We are each going through all kinds of experiences,
according to our karmic path. Can you realize the essence of
what you are going through? You may say, "Why me?" I
respond to you, "Because of you. It's your path to go through."
What occurs in your life, what happens to you, is not a matter
of good or bad. It's not a matter of right and wrong. But so it
is. Buddhist teaching is explained as a way of *chudou,* the
middle path. The Buddhist way is the way of the middle path.
The middle path is not one-sided. It is not extremely negative
or extremely positive. Rather, both sides are unified and
harmonized. *Both ways of responding to what happens to you
are true: If you don't do it, who will? If you did not exist, the
world does not change much.*

The Middle Path creates our way of life into a harmonious
way.

We each have differing capacities to empty our minds, to let go of all ego attachments and "ism's." We differ greatly on such spiritual capacity. I wish someone would make a computer which could judge people for the depth of their spirituality. Such a computer would help us realize that the greater the ability to drop it all leads to a greater ability to see life as it is. The truth manifests itself into life.

YOU CAN TRANSFORM YOUR LIFE

When I was in high school, like other teenagers, I had the desire to be attractive and smart. I blamed my mother that I wasn't as attractive and smart as I wanted to be. I complained to her, "You should have given me a little more brains! Plus I need longer legs. I want to be taller than I am. Why did you make me like this?"

My mother responded, "When I was pregnant with you, I hoped and prayed to have an attractive, smart son . . . But you came out!"

I still remember my mother responding to me in this manner. It made me look at myself as I was, not as I wanted to be. I realized I had such wants, such attachments . . . But so did my mother!

We cannot get away from our attachments. Our fate includes attachments to ourselves and to certain people. It's fantastic! I never get tired of myself. When I spend time with someone I like, an hour is like ten minutes. Maybe for you one day may seem like one minute when you spend time with someone with whom you are in love. In the reverse situation, if

I am with someone I don't like, hate in a sense, thirty minutes is like two hours. Also, I can hold hands with a girl friend and say, "Oh, I love you." Then a very attractive lady may come by and I think, "Wow!" From this view, we each see people and situations in our lives. From this view, we judge people and situations. We cannot escape such attachments. But because of such attachments, we cannot see things as they truly are.

Our egos entangle us. We each need to watch out for our egos. We each think, "What I believe is right." We mostly think what we believe is Universal Truth. But the power of wisdom says, "Hey, relax your shoulders. Drop it! Drop it! See it! Autumn leaves are changing colors."

When you practice meditation, you let your thoughts come and go. Empty yourself, even for one second. Then you can see things as they truly are. Universal Truth is manifested right in front of you. Things are changing and moving on. What are you doing? You are stuck there. Move on, move on.

Also it's better to watch out for myself, not watch out for some other guy. I need to see myself as I am. From this stance, compassion naturally comes out. You will reach out to people and say, "Hi! How are you?" We don't know what will happen tonight, but right now my heart is beating, so I can say, "Take care. Is there anything I can do?" These are true feelings and from these love and compassion come out effortlessly.

In addition to having attachments to our egos and specific people, we also have attachments to concepts with which we fill our brains. You may not like this, but religions are man-made. In fact, all "isms" -- communism, democracy, Christianity, Buddhism -- all come from the brains of men. They are made by people with the best intentions, but still they are devised in the minds of men. We cannot get away from such man-made consciousness. These attachments, too, are our fate. Further, we each view all aspects of our lives from our individual consciousness which is full of "isms."

The truth itself manifests into life. We don't need a word even. The truth is beyond such religions and philosophies and words. It doesn't matter what beliefs you hold. You say, "I believe this because I'm a Buddhist." Or "I believe that because I'm a Catholic." That's fine. But try to see things beyond such identities and classifications.

We each came into this life of human beings with such habits from past lives. Right now we each have a life, a chance to transform the quality of our lives. Go deeper and deeper, transform yourself into the path of awareness, enlightenment even. You may ask, "How can I do this?" We usually think whatever makes me happy *is* my life. On the other hand, we think an experience which makes us miserable and sad is not my life. Instead think of everything that you experience as a gift to you. You can believe that God gave you this life if you want to. To me it doesn't matter who gave us this life. What is important is that it was given to us. Further, take each one of these gifts, these experiences, and learn from them. Use these gifts to nourish, deepen and enrich your understanding of life.

To me whatever I experience is my life itself. *Spiritual practice is totally accepting whatever is happening in my life.* Since we have each one been given this gift of life as a human being, we need to train and guide ourselves.

When a loved one dies, we think a funeral is nothing but sad. Yes, it is sad. But what if you could bring a person who had a painful disease back to life? Would that be happy? We think of occasions like marriage or childbirth as happy. But is married life and raising children nothing but happy? The bottom line of this kind of thinking is that we can learn from sadness as well as happiness.

Hard times, which we all have, are gifts to us. Think to yourself, "What can I learn from this?" I think people who have been sick, faced death or come through other difficulties and crises in life are worthwhile to be my friends. I feel comfortable being with a person who has learned from such experiences. Some people learn from difficult painful experiences. Others do not. This is what makes our lives different. We have very different capacities to offer an empty tea cup. We have different capacities to learn from the experiences in our lives. As we learn more and more, we get so we don't know what is happiness and what is sadness. Then each experience is totally your life, not God's life, not Buddha's life, but your life.

In addition, the questions which occupy your mind have a lot to do with the way you transform your life. The course of your life itself is made up of the questions you entertain in your mind. What questions do you have in your mind? Not God, not Buddha, not the Bible, not Sutras, but you. What kind of questions do you have? I hope you have questions which will push you spiritually. I call these "good questions." These are questions which the more you think of them, the more you learn. The more you learn, the more you feel comfortable and the more you are enriching your life. If you keep a "bad question" in your mind, the more you ask such a question the more you get frustrated and the more uncomfortable you feel. When you share your thoughts on these questions with others, they become uncomfortable also.

Zen Buddhist tradition provides us with koans or questions to ponder. These questions are almost impossible to figure out from our normal knowledge or intellectual analysis. We get stuck. We think, "I can't answer that!" so forget it. If you keep a sincere spirit, some other time, like when a dog barks or when you flush the toilet, Flash! Yeh! You have an answer to the koan.

I think vital questions come from actual life. I find vital questions in the relationship between a man and a woman, in feelings of frustration and joy, in tears and laughter. With each experience I think, "What can I learn from this?   How can I use this experience to become more aware?"

Once we realize our silliness, our stupidity and dumbness, we are in front of the gate and can see the essence of koans. Koan practice does not make sense without your life. Your life itself is koan practice. Your life itself *is* teaching.

Watch your thoughts which arise from your ego as you experience your life. In this way, if you are truly kind to yourself, you are effortlessly kind to others.

DON'T BE FOOLED!

A Zen Master called to himself, "Hey master."
He answered himself, "Yes, yes."
He called back, "You may clearly awaken."
He answered, "Yes, yes."
He responded, "Don't be fooled by any other thing."
He answered, "Yes, yes."

The Zen Master continued to talk to himself with this same dialogue over and over throughout his life. He continued to repeat this dialogue with himself even after he was enlightened. So who was the Zen Master talking to? Who is his master? Another koan to puzzle us!

There is no way to describe who or what he is talking to. But I have to use some words to explain, so I will use Buddhist terminology. Actually there is no so-called Buddhism.

We may say that his master is Buddha Nature, the nature to be awakened, the nature to be a real person or the nature to have a true mind. This is the nature to act spontaneously with true actions and thoughts.

We normally think about reality and constantly make judgements of good and bad, right and wrong, black and white, segregation and discrimination, true and false.

Everyone does this. I am talking about something which is beyond these theories we constantly juggle in our heads.

We each talk to ourselves within our minds, but most of the time we talk with our ego-self and we don't realize it is our ego-self talking. This koan is teaching about ego-lessness, or non-ego. This is a difficult idea for the human mentality to truly understand. It is especially difficult for the Western mentality. In the West the ego is emphasized as self-power or power to overcome any difficulties. Ego-lessness or non-ego means to realize that there is no such isolated thing as an ego; yet, at the same time, to realize we have to have an ego to exist.

In a sense my ego cannot exist without you. This is looking at ego outwardly. To get a concept of how to look at the ego inwardly or psychologically, let's look into Buddhist philosophy which I studied in college a long time ago. Human beings are made up of five aggregates or skandhas: form or the body, perceptions or the body's reactions which show the body is alive, mental conceptions and ideas, volitions or desires, and consciousness of mind. We think that consciousness is the mind, but this is not exactly so. We each have a body or a form which is continually changing. We also each have a mind. This body and mind are temporarily combined to make our existence possible. When we die, this particular body and mind are no longer combined. So, in order for our body and mind to be uniquely combined, we each have an ego. But this particular combination is only temporary, therefore our particular ego is only temporary. Buddha Nature, however, continues to exist.

So now I have given you a psychological and philosophical point of view. But what good is it? Instead of giving you a textbook-like explanation, experienced Buddhist teachers directly ask students to come right into it: "You love your ego. Show it to me."

The student becomes aware of his ego through practice and interaction with the teacher. Buddhist practice may include sitting Zazen, cleaning the temple, setting things up for service, chanting, listening to Dharma Talks and dana practice or the practice of giving and receiving. When students practice, they accept without hesitation whatever comes their way. This is interesting practice for the ego. Through practice students can begin to see how their ego reacts.

You can experience many of these practices here at the Cleveland Buddhist Temple -- sitting meditation or Zazen, cleaning the temple, chanting and listening to Dharma Talks like this one. Right now I am going to talk about traditional dana practice in which students in Japan participate. Such practice is very interesting for one's ego. In dana practice, students walk from house to house. They knock on doors and people who live in the houses offer something, usually something to eat. Whatever is offered, the students accept it without hesitation. They cannot check it or decide if they want it or not. People feel very uncomfortable during this practice. The students think such things as, "Maybe the people spit on this pickle before they gave it to me." Once I asked, "Could this food I received be poisoned?" I was told, "Even that you accept." One of my friends experienced mean treatment during dana practice. People threw coins at my friend and hit him on the head. Also they threw some coins in filthy water. He put his hand in the water to retrieve the coins, bowed, then moved to the next house.

How would your ego react to such practice? During such practice it is interesting to see how our egos work. Outwardly the ego cannot exist without you. I cannot exist without you. The ego is powerful. We are able to function, exist even, because of our egos and their relationships with others. We see things from our egos. This ego view is based on all the knowledge, concepts, experiences, beliefs, faith, opinions, attitudes, thoughts, theories and philosophies which are built-up as we interact with our families and culture. So we think we see things as they are, but we hardly ever do. We actually live much of our lives in beautiful misunderstanding.

Yet, inwardly we can realize that our bodies and minds are combined temporarily because of the five skandhas. We can realize that there is an inherent or inborn way of looking at things, an *a priori* view. I advise you to *drop it!* Meditation helps in this. Tap into the nature from which we can see things as they are, in which our minds are like a white sheet or a mirror. Then we may be able to realize that we are living with a nature capable of enlightenment. Whether it is possible or not, at least be aware that what we think is based on our ego's view.

Realize that you are not definitely right all the time. Do you think you are right eighty percent of the time? Forty-five percent of the time? Twenty-five percent of the time? Perfection hardly ever exists in this relative world. So you need to forgive yourselves and others often. You generally forgive yourselves seventy-five percent of the time and others twenty-five percent of the time.

The Zen Master called to himself, "Hey master."
He answered himself, "Yes, yes."

He called back, "You may clearly awaken."

He answered, "Yes, yes."

He responded, "Don't be fooled by any other thing."

He answered, "Yes, yes."

So don't you be fooled by any other thing. Each one of you has an ego which drives your thoughts, so be aware that this is happening. I am the same. That's the way you are able to get in touch with your true mind. That's the way you are able to get in touch with your awakened mind which is equally given to each of you.

We are all born with it. Then we can enjoy whatever arises from within ourselves. Everything that arises is based on ego. When we realize this, things which arise will not be suffering anymore. This is the interesting part. You will probably still have uncomfortable, even painful moments. But they will not become suffering any more. We may even enjoy these uncomfortable, painful moments.

Watch your thoughts which arise from your ego as you experience your life. In this way, *if you are truly kind to yourself, you are effortlessly kind to others.*

We don't like the suffering in our lives. We say that it is bad, that it causes us a lot of pain and trouble. Yet, it helps us, like the dirty bottom of a pond that helps the lotus flower to go beyond the dirt and become beautiful; like cow shit, which smells and looks bad to us, and yet helps us to produce a beautiful garden that we may enjoy.

BREAKING THROUGH TO THE BLUE SKY

One cloudy, rainy day I was to fly on an airplane from Cleveland to San Francisco. As I waited in line to get my boarding pass, I heard people around me say, "It doesn't look so good. I hope we have a good flight," and, "I hope our flight does not get in trouble."

As we took off, we flew up into the rain clouds. I felt the nervousness of the people sitting around me as we looked out the windows of the plane into the thick gray clouds.

Suddenly, the plane broke through the top of the clouds and into a beautiful, clear blue sky. It was so wonderful! The blue sky was vast, like it would never end. I felt the tension of the people around me subside.

A thought came into my mind, *the blue sky has been there all the time!* The blue sky had not disappeared just because I could not see it as I drove to the airport and as the plane flew through the dark clouds. To see the blue sky, we had to break through some dark clouds. The blue sky had always been there.

I think our life is like this.   In order to see the vast, limitless, endless blue sky of our true nature, we have to break through the gray clouds that are in our lives. As we live our lives, we need to go *through* and *through* and *through!* The true nature of our life is this huge blue sky, but we don't see it. We spend lots of time worrying about the clouds instead of going through them. I think we can use our worries and cares to help us break through to the blue sky of our true nature.

In the so-called Buddhist tradition, the lotus flower is a symbol of enlightenment. The lotus flower is like a water lily; it grows out of the dirty material at the bottom of the pond, and yet produces a beautiful flower that floats on top of the water. Many pictures of Shakyamuni Buddha show him sitting on top of a lotus flower. He became enlightened by breaking through the suffering of his life until he became one with the blue sky, realizing his true nature of becoming a Buddha, an enlightened one.

We don't like the suffering in our lives. We say that it is bad, that it causes us a lot of pain and trouble. Yet, it helps us, like the dirty bottom of a pond that helps the lotus flower to go beyond the dirt and become beautiful; like cow shit, which smells and looks bad to us, and yet helps us to produce a beautiful garden that we may enjoy.

There is no doubt about it; the blue sky is always there. If you look up when the sky is completely filled with dark clouds, you won't see the blue sky, but it is there. So go beyond the clouds and break through, break through. *Go through and through and through, and you will enjoy the blue sky!*

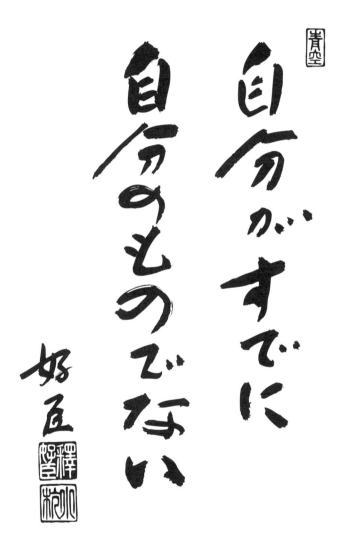

自分がすでに自分のものでない

" Myself has not already been mine"

Zen mind is a mind like a mirror. It reflects you as you are, but when you move away from it, the mirror becomes clear. Be like a mirror. It will reflect dog shit, but the mirror doesn't smell.

WHO BROUGHT YOU HERE?

Sensei: Why did you come here?

Student: For something new.

Sensei: Who brought you here?

Student: Originally, Bobbi.

Sensei: Who is Bobbi?

Student: A friend.

Sensei: Do you go any place that Bobbi tells you to go?

Student: Probably more than I should.

Sensei: Is anyone here for the first time? Who brought you here? You didn't need to come. You could have stayed at home and watched T.V. You could be drinking beer at a St. Patrick's Day Party. But you are here. So who brought you here?

Student: I don't know.

Sensei: You don't know who brought you here, but you are here. I can see by your smile that a question remains in your mind. Bobbi, you brought someone here. Who brought you here?

Bobbi: I thought I would come to listen to you.

Sensei: Are you offering me an empty tea cup? Most of the time we offer a full tea cup. We want the speaker to satisfy our expectations and we think we learn when the speaker says what we expect. But we don't learn much in this kind of experience. We only reconfirm conceptualizations we already have. Who brought you here, Bob?

Bob: It's a mystery.

Sensei: Are you suffering from or enjoying this mystery?

Bob: Both.

Sensei: Sometimes I also both suffer from and enjoy the same phenomenon. Bob is having an interesting experience taking care of two exchange Japanese teachers who don't understand English well. Bob, why is it such an interesting experience?

Bob: I don't know what to expect. I speak a little Japanese. They speak a little English. The rest is confusion. We work it out together. Sometimes we draw pictures.   Many unexpected things happen.

Sensei: If they understood English well, do you think there would be no difficulties? Think about your girlfriend. Do you communicate well with her? She speaks English well. Are the two of you always able to communicate? When you are getting along well with your girlfriend, don't you communicate without words? Also, at times when you are not getting along well, do words help or hinder?

We think in words; we believe that language is the key to communication. But this is not exactly true. In some ways human beings had better communication before we created language. For example, you say, "It's a beautiful day." Others agree, but in agreeing do they all mean the same thing that you do? Another example is two people who say to each other, "I love you." Do they each mean the same? There are many depths and degrees of love. Further, what does, "I love you" mean to each, considering what they do? What will each do because they love the other?

Yes, words can help you create understanding and harmony.   But words also create difficulty and misunderstanding. We are victims of words, conceptions, intellectualization, contradictions, judgements of good and bad or right and wrong. Because of this we get stuck and we hardly ever see things as they are. Yes, the process becomes very uncertain in situations in which we cannot communicate with words, but in some ways it's during such communication that we get to the essence between two people more rapidly.

The bottom line in communication is, "Can I trust this person or not?" This can be felt by intuition; words are not needed. There is something which goes beyond the conceptualized self. I encourage you to get in touch with this something.

Zen tradition and practices help in this. Zen masters use the analogy of the changing states of water to help people understand this something. We wake up in the morning, look out the window and see snow on the ground. The next morning we look out, the ground glistens because it is covered with ice. During the day the sun shines brightly and the snow melts into the ground. This moisture does not remain in the same form. It is constantly changing moment by moment. But our minds get stuck on *It is snow.* Or *It is ice.* Or even *It is melting.* And focusing on words often increases this stuckness.

I often ask people who come to this temple, "Who brought you here?" I continue, "You could have stayed home or gone somewhere else. Yet you came here. *Something* made you decide to come here."

Here is a story that happened to me during my training which may get you closer to this something. I was a student of calligraphy and I asked my teacher, "Is this good?" Usually he corrected my calligraphy, but at this particular time I think he had some kind of intuition and he said, "Perfect." I know my calligraphy cannot be perfect, but later I realized what he meant. I would never be able to draw the same again. I could never duplicate the moment I completed the calligraphy. The calligraphy was not good or bad, right or wrong. Yes, I could compare it with a master's calligraphy and see how poor it was. But this calligraphy and the moments I worked on it can never be repeated again. Yes, my calligraphy teacher was right. The calligraphy in this absolute sense *was perfect.*

Our minds keep busy with attached ideas. Usually these attached ideas are judgements of *This is good* or *Ha, ha, it is better than yours* or *Boo hoo! It's so poor; it's worse than yours.* Getting stuck on this kind of conceptualization affects our communication with others, though it may not affect the words we use. Why can't we truly realize this? The existence of life in the absolute sense is in the here and now. When we truly realize it, we are melting into the something I keep asking about when I say, "Who brought you here?" You can get in touch with something, something which is beyond conceptualized ideas. Things are as they are, which is beyond our judgements of good and bad or right and wrong.

In asking who brought you here, you may say a friend or perhaps you may say a car brought you here. But if we go deeper -- "Who brought me here?" -- we may respond, curiosity, desires, the power of seeking the meaning of life. When you get in touch with it, you will feel comfortable, natural to be what you are. It is easy to misunderstand what I am saying. People often get into a fight when they take the stance, "I am what I am and there is nothing you can do about it!" But if we can get in touch with a sense of egolessness, of non-ego, then we can very naturally be ourselves and accept and respect others as they are.

We think in words and we often think these words are absolutes. We communicate with others using words. But as you communicate with others, be aware of other forms of communication. Notice gestures. Does the person smile or is the person frowning or serious? Does the person feel at ease enough to laugh? What tone of voice is the person using?

Behind such gestures are heart-to-heart feelings. We tap into these non-verbal communications in determining if we can trust another person, if we can be friends.

At times you get in touch with the something I am asking about when I ask, "Who brought you here?" At those times you can be open and blank like a white sheet. It's hard to be like that, but at least you may understand what I'm talking about.

Zen mind is a mind like a mirror. It reflects you as you are, but when you move away from it, the mirror becomes clear. Be like a mirror. It will reflect dog shit, but the mirror doesn't smell.

Who brought you here?

A person who knows sadness may truly know the joy of life. The person who has experienced sickness may feel healthy. A person who is separated from someone may know the joy of togetherness.

PICASSO AND ZEN BUDDHIST TRAINING

Yesterday I went to the Cleveland Museum of Art and saw an exhibition of Picasso. I went with an expert who explained the historical background of each piece we looked at together. I didn't care about what he was telling me. His talking actually bothered me a lot. So I smiled at myself. Rather than thinking about the historical background of each painting, I tried to get the feeling of the pictures. By taking this approach, I could clearly see the process of Zen Buddhist training in Picasso's art work.

First, you see the world around you. You believe that things are as they seem to be to you. But really you see them from your preconceived ideas, or ideas you have gained through living with your family and in our society. You have learned to call a tulip, a tulip, not a carnation. You have learned that the color of a specific tulip is called yellow. This is our shared understanding.

Learning all these labels for the things in our world around us makes communication with others easier. By knowing and using these common labels, we waste less time in communicating with each other. Actually this tulip doesn't care if we call it a tulip or a carnation. So this labeling helps us humans in communicating efficiently, but in another sense it doesn't matter whether this tulip is called a tulip or not. Also the tulip doesn't care if we call it yellow or blue. If we carefully look at and examine this tulip, we can see dark purple and green on the petals -- many more colors than yellow, or maybe we see no colors.

In the same way we think *Let's call God, Buddha; let's call Buddha ,God.* No they are different, you may think. We talk about what we believe, what we understand to be true. In such conversations, we usually end up by implying, "I'm right. You're wrong."

In the second stage of Zen Buddhist practice, we would call this flower a *carnation* instead of calling it a tulip. Much of Picasso's paintings reminded me of the phenomenon of calling a tulip a carnation. This puzzles us, confuses us. Looking at Picasso's paintings is fun, though. So enjoy this phenomenon. What we may call Zen Buddhist wisdom contains such statements as, *A cat is a dog; A cat barks; A dog mews.* Why not call a cat a dog? I think Picasso would agree with this. I say become free from the ordinary view. Others may say Picasso is crazy, but he can see reality from a different stage. And it's fun.

In Buddhist practice, keep going and going. You disappear. I disappear. I become part of all phenomena. No, no, I believe in God; I believe in Buddha, and on and on. *Drop it! Drop it!* Go through and through. On the way to becoming, the mountain becomes a river and a river becomes a mountain. This puzzles us a lot. But why not? Can we call a river a mountain? The mountain streams. The river sits. In an ordinary sense, no!

But keep going through and through. After such a stage, things begin to appear as they are. The mountain *is*   a mountain. The river *is* a river. *I am what I am.* You *are* what you are. At this stage the artistic sense of Picasso is not as much excited, more subdued. As we go through, we realize things are as they are.

Last week Sandra's grandmother was fighting for her life in intensive care. Sandra was sitting here at the temple listening to a Dharma talk. This week Sandra's grandmother is at home recovering, being cantankerous, and Sandra's uncle has died of a heart attack. Things are as they truly are.

So at the beginning we cannot see well. Because of all our preconceived views, we think we see things as they are, but we cannot. With practice we can come to a deep realization, then back to seeing things as they are. But this is an entirely different view, one hundred eighty degrees different.

People who live in the Cleveland area experience snow, cold and then spring comes. People in San Francisco, where the climate is moderate all year-round, don't experience snow and cold as natives of Cleveland do. For people living in Cleveland to say in the spring, "This flower is beautiful," the feelings and impact are so much greater than for someone living in San Francisco where many flowers bloom year-round. I am thankful for coldness and snow of winter leading to the sunshine and flowers of spring. Depth of feelings comes from this type of process. A person who knows sadness may truly know the joy of life. The person who has experienced sickness may feel health. A person who is separated from someone may know the joy of togetherness.

We don't want to be sad, sick, or separated. I say go through the sadness and joy, the sickness and health, the

separation and togetherness in your life. Go through and
through to see things as they truly are.

I think it is an interesting practice to think about: Everything around me is not mine. I'd like to keep my body at age 17, but I can't. I don't want to have a scratchy voice, yet I have one. So even myself is not mine. Since you yourself are not your own, how can you think that you could possess even a baby born to you? A man and a woman in a relationship like to think they possess each other and in thinking this way, they create so many difficulties.

A BUDDHIST MIRACLE

In Buddhist practice we tend to emphasize *seeing things as they are.* We tend not to talk about miracles. But today I'd like to share a Buddhist miracle.

There was a woman named Kisagotami who lost her baby to death. The sadness on the part of a parent who loses his or her child is enormous.

Kisagotami held the body of her dead baby in her arms. She went to a doctor and said, "Can't you make my child well again?" Then she went from one person to another saying, "Can't you do something? Can't you bring my child back to life?"

Kisagotami was frantic. The people around her became scared by her laments. However, she didn't care about what people said about her. The only thing in her mind was to find a way to bring her baby back to life. A man who had heard

Dharma Talks by Shakyamuni Buddha advised Kisagotami to go see the Buddha.

Shakyamuni Buddha observed her carrying the dead baby and knew what had happened. He said to her, "There is a way to get the dead baby's life back. Go and get a handful of poppy seeds from a family who has not been touched by death."

Poppy seeds were common household items, so she began going from house to house. At each house she knocked on the door and asked, "Has someone close to you died?" At each house she received answers like *My child died. My mother died. My grandmother died. My dog died.* The sky became dark, yet she continued to visit house after house. She could not find a single family who had never known death. She decided to return to Shakyamuni Buddha. When Kisagotami saw Shakyamuni Buddha, with tears in her eyes she placed the dead body of her child on a funeral pyre. At that moment she was enlightened. Shakyamuni Buddha spoke to Kisagotami and said, "I cannot possess myself even, so of course I cannot possess another person, even my own child."

Kisagotami realized the truth of life, the law of impermanence, that things are always becoming and moving on. She realized that because we are born, we each shall die. The cause of death is birth. This experience of Kisagotami is what I call a Buddhist miracle.

Did you ever sing a song about God speaking to you? We think God speaks to us from some place, from the clouds maybe. That's a western notion. The eastern approach describes the voice speaking from the inside. But I say let it come in from the outside and go out from the inside. Coming and going. Keep doing it. Then we don't know if it comes from the inside or outside. We see that it is the same thing.

A BEING WITH NO TITLE

Now concentrate. You don't have to be serious yet don't be scattered around. I will not talk too much, nor will we sit too long. So concentrate. Put your whole self together; keep your body and mind together. This does not mean to be tense; rather relax, but focus.

There is a true being who has no title, no name. This being is coming in and out. May you treasure it. May you take care of it. May you nourish it. Be a friend with it and let it grow. This is your treasure.

This true person, who has no name and no title, comes in and out through your senses and organs. If you have not realized him or her, look, look, look! What I am talking about is your treasure. You are living in *it*. Enjoy *it*, be excited with *it*. If you truly realize *it*, your life will be changed and you'll surely enjoy your life.

Zen traditions, Dharma traditions, encourage us to get directly in touch, that is to have a direct consciousness of this being with no title, to realize *it*. In Buddhist traditions when we say to realize, we mean to be aware with our bodies, not just with our minds. You have had hundreds, even thousands of experiences. It's time to enlighten *this something*. Suppose your mother is dying. In Dharma practice, this event is very important. This event will have an impact on your life. Or suppose you are getting a divorce. This, too, is very important concerning the impact this happening has on your life. In fact, whatever is happening in your life is important. It's time to enlighten yourself. Dharma practice consists of direct realization with your body and mind. Dharma practice leads to direct impact. It leads to a realization of the bonding of body and mind. You need to swallow *it*, digest *it* so that Dharma practice is your flesh and blood.

You need to break through conceptualized thinking. We commonly make separations between subject and object. We commonly get excited because the object does not do what we expect or what we wish. Because of this we suffer. As we go through life we each have times of emotional excitement, times of so-called happiness, and times of so-called sadness. As we are involved in Dharma practice, if we break through this dualistic way of thinking about the subject and object, then the subject is the object, the object is the subject. Also, the subject is not itself without the object. When one realizes *this*, one knows what it means to say, "I am the most honorable one in heaven and earth."

If you say, "John is so mean to me," there is a separation of subject and object. One does Dharma practice to break through such separations. An object itself without a subject may realize the theory of egolessness or non-ego. You could say, "Yes, it is. The flower is blooming." In a sense the flower is expanding. Or you may say, "Please be helped." These words, intellectually at least, are free from the separation of object and subject. Another way of saying this is that Dharma practice unifies subject and object. So it is, so I am. So I walk, step by step.

You may exchange conversations with this being with no title. Keep up a discussion with him or her every day and night. You may hear a voice even. These conversations are between the ego self and egolessness. They are conversations with self and selflessness. They are conversations with self and real self. After all, they are conversations with Buddha or God. Through these conversations you will enrich your spiritual life.

Did you ever sing a song about God speaking to you? We think God speaks to us from some place, from the clouds maybe. That's a western notion. The eastern approach describes the voice speaking from the inside. But I say let it come in from the outside *and* go out from the inside. Coming and going. Keep doing it. Then we don't know if it comes from the inside or outside. We see that it is the same thing. Listen to his or her voice. When I say *this voice,* then you think there is a separation between the speaker and the voice, and you fall into the pits of the mistake of separating subject and object. I use the words *self* and *selflessness.* I could also use the words *ego* and *egolessness*, or the words *self* and *real self.* In doing this I am making a mistake because in using these words, I give you the impression that they are two separate entities. The two are the same thing!

We need to break through such a conceptualized way of thinking about subject and object. If you have any questions, keep them. Sit down; drop them all! Your true self is expanded in these moments when you drop them all. Mostly we listen to our ego self. Listen to your true self.

I was staying here in the parsonage last night. I had a dream. My father was in my dream. I said to him, "I don't know why I am doing this. I flew here from Chicago, then I drove to Columbus, now I'm here in Cleveland. In each of these cities I gave Dharma Talks. Why do I do like this?"

My father said, "People in Cleveland learn more than you do, so keep doing it."

Then I heard the cat mew. That was my dream. "What kind of dreams do you dream now-a-days?" is a good question. Dreams tell us what we are thinking about, what level we are living. But don't be too serious or intellectual concerning your dreams.

SINCERITY

There was a Buddhist monk named Gutei (pronounced goo-tae). He was *not* coming into a deeper understanding of Buddha Dharma. One night a Buddhist nun visited the small house where Gutei was practicing Zazen meditation.

The nun walked around the house three times. Then she asked the Zen master, "What is the essence of Buddha Dharma?"

Gutei was surprised.

The Buddhist nun walked away. It was dark. Gutei asked the nun to stay over night.

The Buddhist nun said, "No, I don't want to waste time here in this house with an unenlightened priest."

Gutei was shocked. The next day he decided to go on a trip to seek a teacher whose teachings would deepen his enlightenment. But that night the spirit of his guardian appeared to him in a dream. I don't want to talk in a mysterious way, but when a person is sincere and really concentrates, such things as spirits or guardians do appear.

The spirit of Gutei's guardian said, "Stay here. Don't go on a trip. A great Bodhisattva will visit this house."

So Gutei waited.

A traveling monk stopped by. Gutei was very impressed by him and became his disciple. Gutei practiced under him for three years. He was told to clean the temple and set things in order. He learned chanting and continued to do Zazen meditation.

Gutei asked the traveling monk the question, "What is the essence of Buddha Dharma?" but he got no reply.

I can see the patience of this traveling teacher in *not* answering the question. We usually answer right away and we think this is kindness. But sometimes a teacher is compassionate by being silent. In this way, the teacher is implying, "You will realize it sooner or later. Time has not come yet, but be patient."

Gutei asked again, "What is the essence of Buddha Dharma?"

This teacher finally answered. He raised his thumb up. At this moment Gutei was enlightened.

From then on, whenever Gutei, the monk, was asked something, he answered by putting one thumb up. People were very impressed.

Once Gutei was out of town. One of his students was asked questions by members of the Sangha or community. This student imitated his teacher, Gutei, and put his thumb up. A few people were impressed; most were not.

This student thought, "Hey, this is a good idea. When someone asks me a question, I'll just raise my thumb up."

When Gutei returned to the temple, he overheard students talking about how this student was putting his thumb up when he was asked questions by members of the temple. The next time Gutei was with this student, Gutei abruptly asked this student, "What is the essence of Buddha Dharma?"

With some hesitation, the student put his thumb up. The teacher grabbed it and cut it off!

This is a story, you know. Suppose the story went, "Gutei grabbed his thumb because he was a compassionate man!" What impact would there be? When we face a crisis we become a little more sincere. When a doctor says to you, "You have three months to live," you stop joking about what you have done in your life. When you receive papers from the court that your wife has applied for a divorce, you start looking at the actions you have put into your marriage. We each need such experiences in our lives, that is experiences we cannot ignore. When we face a crisis, we begin to look at how we conduct ourselves.

This is what happened to Gutei's student when Gutei cut off his thumb. Zen teachers have such impact on their students. They behave in ways that seem crazy in the ordinary sense, but there is wisdom and compassion behind what they do. Zen teachers act in harsh ways so that their students will truly look at their actions. Zen teachers act this way so that people will become a little more sincere. I should not explain, but I'm an ordinary person like you, so I talk a lot. Now let's go back to the story about Gutei cutting his student's thumb off.

The student cried when his thumb was cut off and ran out of the temple. The teacher ran after him.

The teacher asked the student again, "What is the essence of Buddha Dharma?"

The student continued to cry. He started to raise his thumb, but there was no thumb! The student was enlightened!

I won't argue whether this is a true story or not. Would a teacher of the Buddha Dharma do something as cruel as cutting off a student's thumb? I am telling this story to show you something. Through losing his thumb Gutei's student became enlightened. Concentrate. What does this mean? What sense of Buddha Dharma could come from a teacher cutting off a thumb of a student? The student then tried to raise his thumb, but there was no thumb. The student was enlightened at that moment. Then the student could begin to truly teach others.

Now keep this story in your mind. Concentrate on what you are doing. At first you cannot help yourself, you will be influenced by preconceived ideas. You may think you have the answer in your mind. But keep this story. Make it your own. Then you can break through the wall of knowledge.

We are always thinking such things
as, "What did you buy? How much
did that cost? What kind of a car do
you drive? What kind of a house do
you live in?" and so on. It is easy for
human beings to become like robots,
for us to lose awareness of a feeling
of connection to other beings or
oneness.

OBON AND MRS. OTA

In the Japanese Buddhist tradition, Obon is a national memorial day. Obon is a time to be united with others, both living and deceased. There are beings other than humans who share our life and make our life possible. Obon is a time to be united with them also. We are united with many others whether we like it or not.

You may make statements like, "I hate my mom," or "I hate the person I work with every day." Whether we like them or not, we are all united in oneness in the spirit of love and compassion. Isn't that beautiful? To me, Obon is very romantic for we are all united together.

In traditional Japan, at Obon time people welcome spirits back into their lives by burning fires in front of their houses. The spirits then stay three days. I say these Obon spirits are thoughtful guests for they do not stay too long. If you had a guest who stayed two or three weeks, you might think, "I wish they would leave sooner. I don't want to cook breakfast every morning!" This is why I think the Obon spirits are very thoughtful.

Also in Japan, Korea and China, people make small boats, write the names of ancestors on the boats and sail these ancestors down a river thinking, "I'll revisit with you a year from now." I think this is a beautiful tradition. It gives us the impact of unity of all beings. We have a chance to express our gratefulness and apologies, even confessions, to these beings. In our modern life, we tend to ignore traditions like this. But traditions like this create warm hearts and heart-to-heart communication.

Obon originally meant to make upside down or to make free from suffering so we can gain enlightenment, so we can gain awareness. At this Obon time I want to share some of the awareness of Marjorie Ota. The Columbus Sangha meets in her house. Mrs. Ota welcomes anyone to the service in her home, white people, black people, as well as Japanese Americans. She does not live in a fancy house. Yet she says, "Welcome, welcome."

I was in Columbus on Friday evening at Mr. and Mrs. Ota's house. Mr. Ota was hospitalized and was going to die. We were at the hospital up until 3:00 a.m. I stayed at their home and came back to Cleveland on Saturday morning.

Around 7:00 a.m., Marjorie said, "Sensei, breakfast is ready." In this crisis situation, she was able to cook breakfast for me. Having coffee together she shared this moment in her life, her wisdom. She said, "Wow, Sensei. I've come through all kinds of difficulties in my life because I always learn from my experiences. I was put in a camp because of racial discrimination. And yet Buddhist teaching says *The past is the past, we learn from the past. The future is yet to come. It is a mystery. We are here at the present time. What am I doing? What am I learning? These are my questions.* Then she paused, and simply said, "The whole thing is your choice, isn't it?"

I was sipping coffee and I said, "Yes, yes indeed."
Marjorie Ota doesn't talk much; she talks with whole feeling.

We can make our lives miserable; we can make our lives enjoyable. How we respond to what happens to us is our choice.

Marjorie Ota took some dishes off the table. She said, "It's very funny, isn't it? It is very simple, but we make it complicated."

"Yes, that's right." Her sharing is much better than my Dharma Talk.

Then she said, "I surely miss my husband. We just celebrated our fiftieth anniversary."

The basic law of Buddhism is the law of impermanence that things are changing and becoming. We have to learn to move along. We call this Dharma. As she sat down to drink more coffee, I thought, "What a great person is Marjorie Ota, that I was able to meet in my life."

How we respond to happenings in our life is our choice. The whole thing is in our hands. Shakyamuni Buddha simply stated, "Everything arises from chita which means heart/mind." Everything arises from our minds. Of course we can use our minds to blame the president, the government, the country, other people, society, our parents, our husband or wife, we can blame and blame and blame. We are born into the life of the human being in such a limited time. As we recited this morning *Hard it is to be born into human life. Now we are living it. Difficult it is to hear the teachings of the blessed one, now we hear it. If we do not deliver ourselves in the present life, no hope is there that we can be free from suffering in the cycle of birth and death.*

Marjorie didn't say all these words, she just said, *"Sensei, it is sad to make this life miserable. The whole thing is our choice."*

内なる声を聞く

好庵

We are each different.   Yet we each
have the opportunity to realize there
is no separate so-called Buddhism.
There is no separate so-called
Christianity.   There is no separate
so-called Judaism.   It doesn't matter
what you call yourself.   When you
walk in the rain, you get wet.   When
you walk in the snow, you get cold.
This is true for all people whether
they call themselves Buddhist,
Christian, Jew or Muslim.

"I AM A NEWCOMER."

Newcomer: I am a newcomer.
               Please give me guidance.

Zen Master: Did you eat breakfast?

Newcomer: Yes.

Zen Master: Did you wash the dishes you used?

               With this, the newcomer was enlightened!

"I am a newcomer.   Please give me guidance."   The
newcomer's spirit is important.   Most people come to this
temple to learn, to grow.   But they are full up to the top of
their heads.   They come with their heads filled with ideas,
knowledge, concepts and such things.   They often have been

crying a lot. Because of these preconceived ideas and their strong feelings, they hardly hear me. So make yourself empty. Then I will share my time and energy with you. I'll assist you. Come here to these introductory meditation classes at least ten times. Then leave and you can do some good in the world.

Something made you come here. You used your time, gas, energy, your car and you are here. That's great! But do not waste the energy that brought you here. I have great respect for your efforts. I have great respect for your intellectual powers. I will listen to what you say. I feel a responsibility. I feel I have something to share. I have poor English, but I'm trying my best. When I feel you are not sincere, I think I might as well be at a Japanese restaurant enjoying myself! Don't get mad and ruffled easily. If you leave mad, it will be hard for you to come back.

It takes enormous energy and time to make oneself like the newcomer in the story at the beginning of this talk. This spirit of the newcomer is saying, "I am a newcomer. Give me guidance." Because the newcomer in the story had this spirit, when the Zen master said, "Did you wash the dishes?" the newcomer was enlightened right there!

You know someone *has* to do the dishes. What would happen if no one did the dishes? What does this story mean to you? Your answer is *your* truth at *this* moment. So it is. Don't be embarrassed about your answer, your truth at this moment. We're changing from moment to moment. We're changing and becoming. Even if you say, "I don't know" to me during two different meditation classes, the second time the energy will be different.

Yes, someone has to do the dishes. This is a reality. We are so conditioned to see things from a rationalistic way of thinking, that we cannot see reality. This a fact of life. In traditional Zen training, students are given three different bowls of different sizes, one for soup, one for rice, and one for pickles. We are each a container with different capacities. Since this is so, why not be the best of yourself? Help yourself along. I ask you, "Did you eat breakfast? Did you wash the dishes?"

We are each different. Yet we each have the opportunity to become free from egoistic thinking. There is no separate so-called Buddhism. There is no separate so-called Christianity. There is no separate so-called Judaism. It doesn't matter what you call yourself. When you walk in the rain, you get wet. When you walk in the snow, you get cold. This is true for all people whether they call themselves Buddhist, Christian, Jew or Muslim.

People get into all kinds of arguments concerning religions. Sometimes there are even wars over religions. In these situations, all religions are like a finger pointing to the beauty of the moon. In all religions we need to look beyond the finger and see the beauty of the moon. Then we can live in harmony and help each other. We can share our wisdom and compassion. We can talk about our faith and beliefs.

But sometimes people are hung up on the finger and are not able to look beyond it. Sometimes we have a discussion about religious beliefs and each side feels uncomfortable. Each side decides to stop talking or to leave the conversation. In this kind of discussion, people are too fixated on the particular religious belief, that is the finger pointing to the moon. Have you ever pointed a finger to the moon around cats and dogs? They will focus on the finger, and never look at the moon. Don't have the mentality of cats and dogs; look beyond the finger to the beauty of the moon. The moon *is* beautiful. This is a reality.

At this temple we practice sitting Zazen, walking and chanting. This practice encourages you to be the best of yourself. It does not matter by which religion you label yourself. It's hard to be this way, but there are two phrases which you need to tell yourself over and over. One is *Drop it!* You need to say this with conviction, with your whole self. Drop your conceptualized ideas about what is right and wrong, good and bad. Then you can see things as they are. The second phrase you need to say is, *Go through and through and through.* Keep marching on, march on through *your* life. We are all on our way to becoming. We are all learning, growing, becoming.

Tonight when we sit, sit. When we walk, walk. When we chant, chant. In this way, you'll be able to see. We are all born in this world. We all have the potential to see reality. Whether you like it or not, good or bad or right or wrong, there is no doubt you are sitting in a chair right now.

Did you eat your breakfast?
Did you wash the dishes?
           So you are enlightened.

I was asked to talk to a man dying of AIDS. This man had requested an interview with persons of all different religions.

When I met him, I couldn't find any words to say. I began thinking, "Should I say, You are OK.? No, that is a lie. He is not OK." So I was quiet. I did feel empathetic.

He broke the silence by saying with some hostility, "I am dying."

I don't know why but I said,"Me, too." He was astonished.

I continued. "Perhaps because I came to see you, I may get in a car accident."

We continued our conversation. The man shed some tears.

I came to visit him several times before he died. When he died, he left all the money he had, $128.00, to the Cleveland Buddhist Temple.

WISDOM!

I said to the cat, "We human beings are the most honorable beings ever created! Do you believe that?"

The cat said, "Meow."

The cat didn't say, "Hey, smart beings. Why are you destroying this planet?" I say this.

Yes, we smart beings are destroying this planet. At the same time we so-called human beings are able to cultivate, advance, and change the quality of our lives. This capacity is given to human beings. One of my teachers used to say, "It's wonderful to be born as a human being."

This capacity we human beings have to change the quality of the way we live is not related to the knowledge with which we fill our heads, nor is it related to what we believe in or the institution with which we are affiliated. This capacity *is* a matter of the extent we are aware of the reality of *this life* and to what we *do* in this life. This capacity is related to the extent wisdom pervades our actions.

Recently someone asked me, "What is the difference between knowledge and wisdom?" My explanation is that knowledge is swallowed, digested. Then it becomes juicy and we shit it. What is left in our bodies and minds is wisdom. But let me give you an illustration from my life of wisdom in action.

Once I was honored to welcome some Catholic nuns to this temple. I have great respect for anyone who comes here. It was a cold, snowy day. I heard their car in the parking lot so I walked to the front door of the temple. When I opened the door I saw the sisters standing in the snow praying.

I said, "Come in. It's snowing."

One sister said, "Quiet."

So I became quiet.

Inside my head I thought, "What the heck. Keep standing and let the snow fall on you."

When they completed their prayer, they walked into the temple. I noticed how humble and well-mannered they were. Then wisdom flashed into my mind in a strange way, at least strange from our usual way of judging. Wisdom can be mischievous sometimes.

I asked, "What were you doing while you were standing in the snow?"

One nun said, "We were praying to God to forgive us for walking into a church different from our own and to give us spiritual strength. We need to learn what is happening in the world so we are here."

I asked, "What did He say?" I was curious about how they would respond.

They became quiet. Then one smart nun said, "Pure prayer does not need an answer."

"Right on! So it is!" I thought. But I know that ninety-nine percent of all prayer is based on the idea of gaining self-satisfaction. People generally pray with the expectation to gain something.

The power of wisdom flashed again in my brain. I said, "If God says *yes* and I say *no*, what will happen? Do you think you can walk into this temple? Even if God says *yes,* I could say, 'No, you can't come in,' but I am welcoming you in. Let's be open and talk about whatever we can share with each other."

These words seemed to bring down the barriers between us and we had such a meaningful, heart-to-heart discussion. We were able to build up great feelings of respect for one another and we enjoyed the open conversation which followed. In this way, the power of wisdom can break through our illusions so that we can see life as it is.

Through our practices we can transform knowledge acquired in our daily life to wisdom. It's kind of scary. In order to gain the capacity to be aware of the reality of your life, you have to be courageous enough to open yourself, to empty yourself. We have been trained from such an early age to continue to fill our brains with knowledge; we think we must keep this knowledge in our consciousness. But I say, "Get rid of it!" How about for four or five minutes a day? Or ten minutes a day? Even though we intellectually think we'd like to be free from conceptualized ideas, we unconsciously keep our minds filled. We are oriented to do this. It is difficult to make things our own. It is difficult not to conceptualize things. The way to gain wisdom is to simply offer our minds as an empty tea cup.

We usually take a step to open ourselves, hesitate, then get scared. We recall some knowledge or orientation and we cling to it. We can't help but see things from our preconceived ideas. Our computer brains continually work to size up the people we meet. We think, "How intelligent she is." Or "How dumb they are." But here, our spiritual practice encourages us to *Drop it!*

Empty yourself. When you see from this perspective, trees become greener. This practice will aid you in gaining the power to get in touch with your intuition. You will become truly aware of such things as the days becoming shorter and shorter.

Here is a koan or puzzle:
Horses have four legs. Chickens have two.

A child could rapidly respond to this, "How stupid. Horses *do* have four legs. Chickens *do* have two legs."

This is a perfect answer. How would you respond? I empty myself. Then I could say to the cat, "Yes, today human beings are destroying the planet we live on. But we human beings have the capacity to come right into this koan or puzzle. We have the capacity to change the quality of the way we live."

You are matured enough, educated enough, experienced enough, spent money enough and aged enough. Instead of using the concepts of sin and being positive to guide your behavior, can you be truly yourself by listening to your own true mind and heart? Listen to what brought you here. You may call it sincerity or nobility.

CAN ONE BE POSITIVE?

Sensei: One of you sitting here tonight called me on the phone today and said, "I was told to live positively. How can I be positive? What do you think?"

Student: Understand the nature of our lives.

Sensei: Anyone else? Anything you say is fine. Please get rid of the habituation of judgements of good and bad and right and wrong. Here you can be yourself. This does not mean you can destroy things and behave in a manner that disturbs others. But be truly yourself.

Angie: Things are constantly changing. Even if you experience something unpleasant, it won't last long. However, there is always something to be positive about.

Sensei: Thank you. We all can share. Often, silence
            shares a lot. A person who is silent, attentive,
            shares a lot. Anyone else?

Peter: Something negative, just forget about it.

Sensei: Can anyone come up with words which are free
            from positive and negative? Words which point to
            a way of living that is not positive and not
            negative. Let's come up with more words whose
            concepts are free from the concepts of positive and
            negative.

Students: Detached. Acceptance. Non-attachment.
            Be like a mountain. Freedom. Just be.
            Tolerance.

Sensei: This afternoon I listened as one of you talked on
            the phone. I have a way of catching the feelings
            now-a-days. I listened to the words you were
            saying, yet at the same time I listened to your
            feelings.

As I listened I smiled to myself. I chuckled. You asked,
"Why are you laughing?"

I said, "Well, because you are stepping into a so-called
positive way of living right now."

"How can I be positive?" you asked.

I smiled to myself because just by asking the question, you
were already living in a positive way. I say this because you
were looking at yourself. This is quite dynamic. Most of the

time we cannot see ourselves. But as you talked on the phone, you could see yourself as you said, "I'm not positive." I heard sincere feeling. Sincerity is already taking one step into action. When you entertain such a question, you are seeing yourself.

We are all stupid, you know. But a wise man realizes his stupidities. A stupid person never realizes how stupid he is. In fact, a stupid person who thinks he is wise is dangerous. When you realize what we are talking about in regard to yourself, you are one step into wisdom. Spiritual maturity involves learning to be careful with your stupidities. It involves watching out for yourself and others.

I watched TV and a beautiful speaker emphasized, "Be Positive! Be Positive!" The speaker asked everyone to say together, "Be Positive!" From watching such a show, you may think, "I have to live positively. I have to stop being so negative." But I say it is extremely easy to become a victim of concepts.

Peter: A victim of our own concepts or other people's concepts?

Concepts are created by others and by myself. Most of the time I create concepts myself from what people tell me or from beliefs I'm told. *The point is that we can watch what goes on in our minds so that we will not become a victim of concepts.*

Concepts are very uncertain. Positive? What is positive? How positive are you? Some people may look at the way I live and think I am living positively. I don't bother and harm others. I don't destroy things. Is that living positively?

We are all victims of concepts. We all suffer from this affliction. Universal Truth is right here, yet we all look somewhere else and without realizing it, we have become a victim of concepts. Buddhist wisdom emphasizes a way to be free from concepts of positive and negative. Rather than worrying about whether you are being positive or negative, be truly yourself at each moment. This way of living is more than positive and more than negative. I've never had the concept of trying to be more positive or more negative. I'm saying, "Watch out! Watch your thoughts. Don't be a victim of such concepts."

Related to "being positive" is the concept of guilt and sin. Many people are a victim of this concept. The idea of sin may be needed for some people to live harmoniously with others. This concept keeps some people from harming others. But you have come here to the Cleveland Buddhist Temple. You are matured enough, educated enough, experienced enough, spent money enough and aged enough. Instead of using the concepts of sin and being positive to guide your behavior, can you be truly yourself by listening to your own true mind and heart? Listen to what brought you here. You may call it sincerity or nobility. Call it whatever you like.

One person gets excited and criticizes the temple and me. Others have a deep sense of appreciation that this temple is here, that I have been here for fifteen years, that Zen Shin Sangha is here. These people are not negative or positive; they are the way they are.

I have talked about so-called "positive" and "negative" for about twenty minutes. You have all been listening. But the impact on each one of you is very different. It's not my responsibility, though. It's yours.

I say *blue sky* as I have frequently. The way each of you receives it is entirely different. I do what I can. The way you receive what I say is related to your sincerity and to the way you nourish yourself. This has created the energy that is your life at this present moment.

At the same time, you have such a treasure -- the energy that brought you here. This energy could change the quality of your life. Use this energy to be aware of each of your life experiences. This energy then can continue to the next moment of life, and the next and the next, so that this moment is eternal. This is the way of enlightenment.

So what part can human beings play in this As It Isness? So what is my part in all this? Words, ideas, information . . . we burden our minds and live with them. They frequently cause problems in our relationships with others. What we do is the key.

MIND SHADOWS

An old Buddhist monk wrote Chinese characters for *mind* on the gate, windows and walls of his hut. So when he looked around, he saw the Chinese character or word for *mind* all over. A Buddhist monk friend visited him, saw all the characters or words for *mind* on everything in the hut and said, "No, the gate should have the character for *gate* on it; the window should have the character for *window* on it; the wall should have the character for *wall* on it." Later, a third monk visited the old monk, saw the character or word for *mind* written on everything in the hut and said, "The gate manifests itself without a character or word, so does the window and the wall. You need no signs at all."

This story is a koan, a question which puzzles us. The monk didn't talk or intellectualize about why he wrote the character or the word for *mind* on the things in his hut, he just did it. I want you to come into this puzzle with your whole self with actual experience, not just intellectual understanding.

By writing the character or word for *mind* on things in his hut, this monk was reminding himself of the *mind only* Buddhist teaching: all things are created by the mind. *Things as you see them are only shadows of your mind.*

The Dhammapada says *All that we are is the result of what we have thought. It is founded on our thoughts, it is made up of our thoughts. If a man speaks or acts with pure thoughts, happiness follows him like a shadow that never leaves him. "He abused me, he beat me, he defeated me, he robbed me." For those who do not harbor such thoughts, hatred will cease.*

I can see that my life is like an echo. When my actions and words say, "You are stupid," it echoes back to me, "YOU ARE STUPID." If I am thoughtful and kind to others, people are thoughtful to me.

But how can I make my life an echo which reverberates thoughtfulness and kindness? An interesting question, isn't it? Let's look further into the koan with the three Buddhist monks.

The monk's friend pointed out the gate is a gate, the window is a window, and the wall is a wall. We need to understand this, acknowledge that objects like the gate, window and wall, and people in our lives, are as they are. We need to appreciate them as they are.

Snow is falling. Cars are passing by. Someone is killed by a car passing by. My dog is barking. You are crying. You feel joy. You get mad. Crocuses are blooming. These are all manifestations of *As It Is-ness*. Buddhists call the manifestation of *As It Is-ness* Buddha Dharma. Or you might call it a spiritual force within each of us. We question, "How can we tap into this spiritual force within us, this *As It Is-ness*?"

We think. We hear. We talk to others. Sometimes we each make mistakes in what we say. But communication is built up as we interact. Similarly so-called "education" is built up through reading, listening to lectures, completing tests and writing papers. More subtly prejudices and attitudes toward others are built up as we live with our family and friends. We form many prejudices and attitudes toward others whom we perceive as different from us. We talk, talk, talk. We build up knowledge, more knowledge and more knowledge. We have attitudes and when we listen to a speaker who has similar attitudes as we do, we say, "He is a good speaker," because he agrees with our preconceived ideas. But in this case we don't grow much.

Zen takes a severe stance concerning all this talk, knowledge and attitudes in which we have put so much effort. *Drop them all!* You think, "But it took so much of my time and energy to learn so much. Plus education is expensive in this day and age!" But this information, education, knowledge and attitudes are shadows in your mind. You need an empty mind to melt into *As It Is-ness.* The third monk was saying that truth, *As It Is-ness* manifests itself, so there is no need for signs or *mind shadows.*

As we sit or do Zazen together, I emphasize that you are the only one with your life. I emphasize that the truthfulness of the existence of your life is beyond conceptualized ideas of good and bad or right and wrong. You may think, "Yes, I have truth. I have the truthfulness of my life." But by thinking in this way, you attach yourself to this concept and you miss the essence of its meaning. So even truth, if attached to, becomes a concept and a burden which we carry around in our minds. Even a Universal Truth can become a shadow in our minds.

So what part can human beings play in this *As It Is-ness?* So what is my part in all this? Words, ideas, information -- we burden our minds and live with them. They frequently cause problems in our relationships with others. *What we do is the key.*

I've been living in this country for twenty-five years, and I've always been able to become friends with others. I frequent an informal breakfast/lunch restaurant near the temple. I am called China Man by the waitresses.

When I was at this restaurant, the waitress called to me, "China Man."

I smiled and said, "Hi, how are you?"

A man sitting in a nearby booth overheard our conversation and looked questioningly at me. He advised her, "You shouldn't used such racial language with him." He thought that the waitress had insulted me by calling me China Man. In his mind he was sending the message to the waitress, "You are discriminating against this man." When I finished the bowl of soup, the waitress gave me another bowl of soup. The stranger was shocked; he was thinking, "What kind of relationship is this? The waitress calls him China Man which is an insult and then gives him a free bowl of soup!" The stranger's idea of racial discrimination was a shadow in his mind.

So how can you get in touch with *As It Is-ness*? What is your part in all this? What can you do right now in your life? *Things as you see them are only shadows of your own mind.*

*Two small children are fighting over a
cup.
One says, "It's the Zen master's tea
cup."
The other says, "No, it's the Zen
master's coffee cup."
"No. You are wrong!"
"No. You are wrong!"
They kick and hit each other. In the
foray, the cup falls to the floor and
breaks and becomes small pieces of
ceramic. The Zen master stamps on
the ceramic pieces and they become
powder. A potter sweeps up the
powder, adds water and uses the
mixture to make a bud vase. The Zen
master wonders, "How long will this
go on?"*

WHY DOES BODHIDHARMA HAVE NO HAIR?

Zen Master Waku An asked, "Why does Bodhidharma
have no hair?"

I encourage you to walk into Bodhidharma. Then the
conceptualized view of Bodhidharma will disappear and you
will believe you have disappeared. Or you could say you both
melt into one taste of the ocean. And there is *no hair*.
Bodhidharma has no hair at all! So what does *hair* mean?
What is this koan trying to teach us? What is Zen Master Waku
An trying to awaken in us?

Tonight I will talk about this koan. I will talk about what
it means intellectually. Listen tonight. Then, between now and
the next meditation class, think about how you could explain

this to a friend. The friend doesn't have to know anything about Buddha Dharma. You need to be friendly and nice to your friend, but most of the time we are really confused. How can you explain the content of the koan to make your friend understand? What is *hair*? What does *hair* mean? You don't have to mention the word hair or Bodhidharma or Buddha Dharma. Rather try to communicate the awareness Zen Master Waku An is trying to get across. What is hair? Bodhidharma obviously has *no hair*. It makes sense. At first I thought it didn't make sense.

When we hear Bodhidharma right away, we picture the man Bodhidharma with his beard and a lot of hair. We know he has lots of hair. The obvious question should be, *Why does he have so much hair?* Or *Why does he have that large beard?* The answer could be *He likes lots of hair.*

But Zen Master Waku An asked, "Why does he have *no* hair?" Maybe he is not talking about the man who brought the Buddha Dharma from India to China. Maybe he is not talking about this man's physical body but rather the essence of Bodhidharma: His entire life was the manifestation of the Buddha Dharma. His life was the manifestation of *As It Is-ness.* The body or form of Bodhidharma had lots of hair; Buddha Dharma, the manifestation of *As It Is-ness*, has no hair at all.

We are born as human beings. Then we are given all kinds of orientations. We have a consciousness to be wise and smart. We seek and attain education and knowledge like merit badges. We accumulate concepts and judgements of good and bad and right and wrong. We see, hear, and think with all this as filters. When Jan says, "That is good," she means something different from me when I say, "That is good." When we agree, we do not realize our perceptions are different. In this way we create some kind of understanding. The depths of realization are very different, yet we firmly believe our perception is absolute and perfect. Further, we human beings tend to look for concepts and ideas which will fit into their preconceived notions. Then when a talk fulfills our expectations, we say, "He's OK. He makes sense. He's a good speaker." What we mean by this is that he says what I think; he reaffirms *my* ideas which are absolute and perfect.

The Zen response to all these judgements, concepts and knowledge is *Drop them!* How can I? you think. I listened to my parents, I went to school and listened to teachers for many hours, I studied so hard, I had so many experiences. How can I drop them all? I made such an effort to accumulate them.

You didn't have to come here tonight to practice Zazen, chant and listen to this Dharma talk, but you are here. Your thinking is already set up. You could just keep adding and adding and adding onto it. But we cannot deny the true nature within us to seek some meaning. This nature brings us to learn and to practice. We each come to this temple to seek some meaning, to practice.

We each have been impressed, oriented, habituated and convinced that without any doubt what we see, hear and think is absolute. We believe that what we see, hear and think is the right way to see, hear and think. Ordinarily we think this way. Everyone does. Actually what we see, hear, and think is based on knowledge, experience, false consciousness, concepts, subjectivity, objectivity, beliefs, our faith, judgements of good and bad or right and wrong. Zen encourages us to take all these and *drop them all*!

As followers of the Buddha Dharma, we realize that what we see, hear and think contains limitations and incompleteness. At least we can be aware that this is true. This view, a realization that what we think consists of limitations and incompleteness, is so-called Absoluteness, Is-ness, Suchness, Thusness. Zen encourages us to see, hear and think of people and events in our life from an *a priori* consciousness or an inherent, inborn consciousness.

Zen practice says *Drop it! Drop them all!* Zazen meditation will take care of it. Dharma is so explained in the Heart Sutra. . . .

Remember, Dharma is fundamentally Sunyata. No birth, no death, nothing is defiled, nothing is pure. Nothing can increase, nothing can decrease. Hence, in Sunyata, no form, no feeling, no thought, no volition, no consciousness, no eyes, no ears, no nose, no tongue, no body, no mind, no seeing, no hearing, no smelling, no tasting, no touching, no thinking, no world of sight, no world of consciousness . . .

No hair!

When you come right into the vast openness of Sunyata, you lose your ego. Yes, your ego is power. Especially in this modern life we think we need ego power. But through this practice, your ego can tap into the universal ego, limitlessly, boundlessly. You can feel the way Bodhidharma felt. The events and moments in your life are manifestations of Dharma. My life is Dharma itself. Dharma has no hair. Hair is all the knowledge and judgement we have built up from the moment we came out of our mother's womb, using our vocal cords with all our might, filling our lungs with air and yelling, "Yah!" taking a breath of worldly air. We begin to breathe. We begin to acquire knowledge. We begin to believe that what we see, hear and think is absolutely right.

Zazen practice can help you to see, hear and think about events and moments in your life with an *a priori* view, with an inherent or inborn wisdom. You may wonder, "How could I see before I was born as a human being?"

At birth my voice came out; I didn't hesitate and neither did you. At the moment of birth, each of us did not feel self-conscious because of such ideas as our mother and father are poor and our yelling may embarrass our parents. At the moment of our birth each of us manifests truth itself. When we are born, we have built up no experiences, no knowledge, no judgements, no beliefs.

Beliefs cause such differences. Some people can't talk to each other because they have beliefs which differ. Many believe *theirs* are the only true beliefs and everyone else is wrong. They don't want to associate with people who are wrong. That is *Hair*.

Here is a story that I made up which shows the kind of trouble *hair* or attachments cause as we live with each other.

Two small children are fighting over a cup.

One says, "It's the Zen master's tea cup."

The other says, "No, it's the Zen master's coffee cup."

"No. You are wrong!"

"No. You are wrong!"

They kick and hit each other. In the foray, the cup falls to the floor and breaks and becomes small pieces of ceramic. The Zen master stamps on the ceramic pieces and they become powder. A potter sweeps up the powder, adds water and uses the mixture to make a bud vase. The Zen master wonders, "How long will this go on?"

It's funny to think that two human beings would fight over such a small distinction as, "It's a coffee cup." "No, it's a tea cup." But we do this all the time. Have you ever pointed to a dog in front of a young child and said, "Pet the cat." The child will get upset. We each have egos like this. We are sure that this is the Zen master's coffee cup and not his tea cup! Even nations act this way.

Each of these children thinks their view is right. They do not realize there are other views or that the cup whose label they are fighting over will at some point change in form. *We are all like these children, believing their view is correct.* Believing this is *having hair.* Believing this is not realizing that we have *attachments in our minds.* We each need to realize that, "I have hair or attachments." How can you realize this as you live your life?

Buddha Dharma, truth, has no hair at all. By puzzling over this koan, "Why does Bodhidharma have no hair?" you can expand within yourself. I encourage each one of you to experience this koan through your life. Then this koan will be yours, not Zen Master Waku An's, not Bodhidharma's, not anyone else's but yours.

Buddha dharma has no hair. Now at least intellectually you can understand it. Write it down on a piece of paper. Swallow the paper. Digest it.

At the next mediation class, you can explain how you could make a friend understand this koan. Most teachers learn a lot when they start teaching. When you try to make your friends understand, you learn a lot. You can gain a deeper and deeper understanding.

Why does Bodhidharma have no hair? No hair at all. Yet we let hair grow and grow.

About 30 years ago I had the opportunity to go to Brasilia, the newly built capitol of Brazil. The airport was quite large with many places for different airlines, yet they only used two of the places. I said to an attendant, "There are only two places being used in this big airport!" The attendant said, "In 50 years, this airport will be bustling with people. Brasilia will be a thriving capitol."

Such an interesting consciousness of time this attendant had. We usually don't think this way.

SHINKO AND HIS ANXIOUS MIND

I don't think Buddhist teachings have any hidden teaching. Rather Buddhism teaches ordinary things. This may disappoint you. You may want something mysterious or you may want a miracle.

I was at a wedding reception yesterday. A lady sitting next to me said, "How can I take care? I have to face so many problems at work and at home?" As the woman continued, *problems, problems, problems* kept coming up in her rapid stream of talk. While she talked, I felt her nervousness; her voice was high pitched.

Most of the time when people ask questions like this, they have their own answer already. But when we keep thinking our preconceived ideas over and over, we don't learn much. When this lady asked me the question, I was quiet. Instead of rushing to push myself to say something right away,

I waited to let wisdom manifest. That's one thing I learned from meditation practice.

I asked, "Why do you call them problems? Please think about this."

She slowed down a bit and said, "That is a good question. I never thought about that before."

As I listened to her I agreed, there is much stress in our so-called advanced way of living. I think most of us living in America today ask, "How can I become free of this stress?" Here is a story which may help us with this question.

The legend says that in the sixth century in China, Bodhidharma sat toward the wall for nine years. From our standards we may think he was either stupid or he didn't have much to do. Here in the twentieth century American culture, we often can't meditate for even ten minutes.

One night a true seeker named Shinko came to see Bodhidharma and Bodhidharma did not respond. Finally, Shinko cut off his arm at the elbow. He did this to show his determination to Bodhidharma. Who knows if this story is true or not.

With this demonstration of seriousness, Bodhidharma looked at Shinko and asked, "What do you want?"

Shinko said, "I have been practicing to find peace of mind. Yet I cannot settle my mind. How can I settle my mind?" Shinko was stressed and anxious.

Bodhidharma said, "Bring your unsettled mind to me and I will heal it."

So Shinko went into deeper and deeper practice to find his anxious, uncertain mind. He could not grasp it to take it to his teacher. In his frustration he went back to Bodhidharma and said, "I cannot find my unsettled mind to bring it to you."

Bodhidharma smiled and said, "So now I've healed you."

Then Shinko was enlightened. He realized there was not such a thing as his unsettled mind, but that he himself created such anxiety with his body and mind. He knew that there was nothing but his life itself.

Here is an intellectual discussion of Shinko trying to find his unsettled mind and what happens as we think about our *problems* creating feelings of anxiety. The mind is not the brain. If the mind is not here, nor there, so where is it? The mind arises from the causes and conditions surrounding it. Some of the conditions are created by the filters through which we view our life. If you would ask children in Hawaii and children in Chicago to draw the waves, the children familiar with Lake Michigan would draw smaller waves than the Hawaiian children familiar with the Pacific Ocean. From the conditions we are used to we judge happenings as *I like it* or as *It is a problem.* Then our minds try to fix the problem right away. Yet all these happenings or so-called problems are changing and becoming. So these situations we call *problems* are actually always changing.

Consciously and unconsciously we separate from situations in our life and we think of them as *problems.* I say the more we have distance between ourselves and situations which we think are *problems*, the more we will suffer. The less distance, the less we will suffer. Many people are looking for God's love and support either consciously or unconsciously, yet their thinking puts distance between God's love and themselves. Yet these same people are seeking and they aren't conscious that they live in God's love itself. In the Buddhist tradition, we say we are living in the immeasurable wisdom and compassion of the cosmos. The cosmos in this tradition is known as Amida

Buddha, Infinite Compassion and Wisdom. If you can feel this, then you put less distance between yourself and *the problem.*

As I left the wedding reception, I kindly told the lady to ask herself, "Why do you call it a problem?" You can do the same thing.

Four

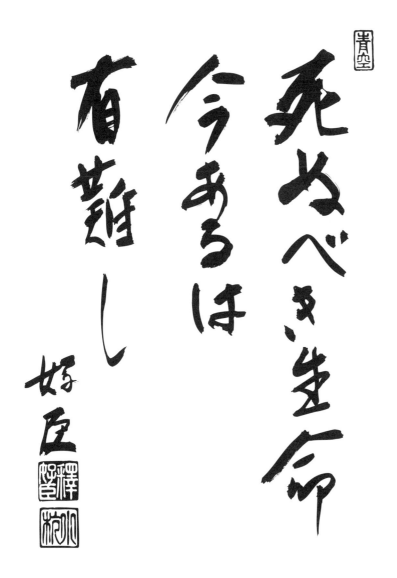

"The life which is dying is existing
right here now and is grateful"

Man is not learned because he talks much. If patients are cured by a doctor, then is the doctor learned? Or is it that patients are able to heal themselves with a push from the doctor? So I think you had better practice more than hearing my talk. I smile at myself a lot lately. I am expected and obliged to talk like this, to talk like this is my karmic path. That's why I do like this. When I talk, I build up hope. The more I talk, the more there is a possibility of creating more sickness in people, so I smile. I think, "What are we human beings doing?"

TO KNOW IS DELUSION;
NOT TO KNOW IS IGNORANCE

A student asked a teacher, "What is the way or path?" The teacher said, "If you seek the way, you will become apart." The student was puzzled. He said, "If I do not seek the way, how do I know?"

The teacher said, "To know is delusion. Not knowing is ignorance." The student queried, "So what should we do?"

We go to one workshop and then another. We use time, energy and money. To know is delusion. Not knowing is ignorance. So what are you doing? Open up to the vastness, one step at a time. As I share in another talk, we get hot sometimes, we get cold sometimes. We feel miserable sometimes. We feel content sometimes. Don't be apart from these.

Open up to vastness. Here are some examples of this way of being. A mother is feeding her baby while you are talking. She says, "Would you please be quiet?" We say spontaneously to someone, "I love you." I was talking this morning to Ken who just yesterday lost a dear friend. Even though this happened to him, he is downstairs this morning chopping vegetables for the meal after the service.
Here is a poem I like.

Spring flowers.
Summer rain.
Autumn harvest moon.
Winter snow.
Any season is a good season.

In the winter time we say, "Cold, cold, cold." When you do this, remember this poem. We think we are enlightened or will be enlightened. We think we are happy or we wish we were happy. The more we think, the more we are away from reality. When we keep thinking we are attached to the path in this way, then we feel stress, pressure. The way or the path is not a matter of knowing or not knowing. Knowing is delusion and not knowing is ignorance. When I have reached the way, the way is as vast as life and death.

How are you taking care of your Buddha Nature? It's natural to be enlightened. We are living in the exact right place and the exact right time. There is no other place, which means any place is a meaningful place. You don't have to travel around. Simply look at your life, at your family or loved ones, or those around you. Keep walking, walking; this is the right place and the right time.

Why did Ken's dear friend die? The cause of death is birth. Life manifests itself here, now. Practice love, compassion, wisdom. You are the only one with your life in the entire universe. Eternal life is at this moment. So? So? So? How are you taking care of this life? Sometimes, as well as extending sympathy, I ask, "Are you enjoying it?" Keep sharing your life with others. Then one day you will smell the flowers. To know is delusion. Not to know is ignorance. Ordinary mind is the way.

If you feel satisfied that you know this, then you are stupid. We are all victims of thoughts, so empty your mind. Analyze it. Try to understand. Think about it as you walk down a hall, as you sit on the toilet. Wash dishes, argue, get excited, despair. Don't be apart from it. Perhaps there will be a moment when someone touches you and you understand. We are all victims of thoughts.

Ordinary, harmonious, intuitive mind is the way.

We have been oriented to think that eternity is beyond this world. This thinking separates now and eternity. The way of wisdom encourages us to see eternity as part of the present, as part of *this moment right now.*

Yesterday and tomorrow do not make sense without today. This moment does not make sense without the last moment or the next moment. Get it? Already when I say *Get it?* then that present is past. Last moment, this moment, next moment. Moments are changing with such speed. We hardly see it.

Yesterday is past. It's history. Tomorrow is the future, unknown. We often have hopes for what will happen in our lives tomorrow, but each one of us could have a heart attack tonight and thus be dead tomorrow. However, today is the link between yesterday and tomorrow. Today, this moment is real. Thus, now is the moment of eternity.

Let's look further at this idea of making the most of the eternal moment through the koan *Ordinary Mind is the Way*. We worked on this koan during our recent sesshin. I will try to communicate this koan through the logic of language, but I want you to take it into your everyday life. Don't be like an impoverished professor of economics; don't just intellectually know about this koan, enrich your life with it.

The Japanese word, *heijyo shin,* from which ordinary mind is translated literally means *ordinary mind, harmonious mind, intuitive mind.* In the story which goes with this koan, Joshen asked his teacher, Nansen, "What is the Way?"

Nansen said, "Ordinary Mind is the Way. This morning you got out of bed. You washed your face. You had breakfast. You worked. You had all kinds of experiences."

Joshu said, "Yes. But should I concentrate on figuring out the Way?"

The master said, "If you look for and concentrate on *What is the Way?,* then you are going further from the Way."

Joshen persisted in asking questions, "If I do not look for the Way, how do I find the Way?"

The teacher responded, "The Way does not belong *to know* or *not to know.* If you try to calculate and figure out the Way, you will start having the consciousness that you know the Way or that you don't know the Way. Then you will fall into illusions."

The teacher was trying to explain how knowledge can become poisonous and ruin Joshen's experiencing the essence of the moment. He was telling Joshen to *Just live*, rather than using his knowledge to try to figure out how to find a special way of life.

Simple, direct mind is very powerful. Experience what you are doing right now. Living this way is like opening the skies that surround you. To have a simple, direct mind, don't ask *Why?* Don't think *Why did this happen to me?* Don't worry about what will happen tomorrow or try to control what will happen tomorrow. We think we can solve problems by asking such questions and considering all possibilities. But the more you ask such questions and fabricate all possible happenings, the more complicated things become. Don't ask. Simply feel rain on your cheeks. Simply listen to the person sitting across from you. Simply do what you need to do.

As human beings we are able to see, think, hear, feel and act during each eternal moment of our lives. Become aware of each experience in your life. Abundant opportunities are given to each of us.

Ordinary Mind is the Way.
Harmonious, intuitive Mind is the Way.
Make this our life. Make it your flesh and blood.

This is your treasure. After all, you are the one who takes care of your life. You have such a precious life which can't be repeated again with the same conditions and situations. You have one life to live. It sounds like a soap opera. It is indeed. One life to live. And it's all in your hands. Don't say *My life is in God's hands or in Buddha's hands.* These are irresponsible words. Think *It's all in my hands.* Then God will be pleased to hear about your life.

*Our sorrow consists not in the
shortness of life, but in our
inability to make supreme use of
the present moment.*

WHEN A LOVED ONE DIES

John died. I said to John's loved ones, "I believe John lived his life with his ability and with his might in his karmic path. He shared his life with his family and friends when things were good or bad or sad or happy. I enjoyed playing golf with him."

When a loved one dies, I extend respect to the family and friends who shared his joys and suffering. Also I am sure that John's truthfulness, wisdom, kindness, patience and smile will never die, but will shine in our hearts and give us the light of wisdom.

I also admire the family for deciding on a service which is practical and meaningful. When someone we care for dies, we have strong feelings. We don't know what words to say. But when we come to the temple we light candles and offer incense and chant sutra. Our mood becomes less agitated; we settle down. A peaceful feeling is created. Then the feelings which arise at the loss of a loved one are somewhat less difficult for us. When our minds are calmed, we can become open to the reality of life.

I could say hundreds of beautiful words to comfort you in your sadness. You may feel security and satisfaction at the time of a loved one's death when hearing and thinking about many ideas from the various religions. But I encourage you to develop the ability to face death as a part of life, and from there you may overcome your sadness and learn to take care of your life.

I have heard people say so many times, "I can't believe it! I just talked to him on the phone last night." Or they say, "I had dinner with him two days ago! I can't believe it!" For twenty-five years as a minister I have heard people say countless times, "I can't believe it!" It doesn't matter whether you believe it or not, it happened. It's beyond our beliefs. The truth always manifests itself beyond our beliefs.

It is very difficult to accept the reality of the death of a friend or family member, especially when the loved one dies at the age of forty-seven. Is forty-seven young? Young and old are interesting concepts. What is young and what is old? Ten years old is *old*! Just ask a five year old. Forty-seven is younger than eighty-five. So this man died at the age of forty-seven, yet reality is quite beyond our grief and words. You see, whatever we say or however we express our emotions, the reality is very cruel. And so it is, he died at the age of forty-seven.

In our western culture we don't look at such things as burned bodies and the remaining bones. Rather we observe the body in an embalmed state and then cover the body up in a casket. We say, "He went to heaven." But we are kind of scared to see the reality of it, which is interesting.

Rennyo Shonin, a priest of Shin Buddhism, stated in one of his epistles, "In the morning we may have radiant health; in the evening we may be white ashes. When the winds of uncertainty strike, our eyes are closed forever. When the last breath leaves our body, the healthy colors of our face are transformed and we lose the appearance of radiant life. Our loved ones may gather around and lament, but to no avail." That is a very cruel message, isn't it? When a person dies, loved ones can do nothing to bring the person back to life. Renyo wrote further, "When such an event occurs, the body is sent into an open field and cremated, leaving only white ashes. What a sad plight." As was the custom in Japan in the past, the family waited until the cremation was over, then they picked the bones and placed them one by one into a box. This aids the family in realizing the death of the loved one.

We will have questions unless we face the reality that our friend or family member has died. Renyo is telling us to develop our ability to see our life as it truly is, to see the changing nature of human life, to accept the reality as it comes with a truthful mind. We tend to see things, including the death of a friend or relative, with our convenient mind or egoistic mind. We even get angry at the person for leaving us by dying. With time, a truthful mind will accept things as they truly are.

Ikkyu, a Zen priest, said, "It is good to die when we die. It is good to live when we live." That's all! Behind such a simple message, he's saying *Hey, you! While we are living, why not learn to concentrate on living?* Even though we may want to die, we will not die until the time comes. Conversely, even though we may not want to die, we will die when the time comes.

John died at the age of forty-seven. We may think this is too young to die. We generally think that. Even I think that, you know? What age is a good age to die? I asked a lady in our temple who was 103, "Isn't it hard to live up to 103?" She said, "Yes." The saddest thing she had to go through was facing the death of her own child. For parents to face the death of their own child is extremely difficult. So I don't know if living that long is good or bad. She was in good health and cared for by her family members. She shared her wisdom and compassion for 103 years. But until the time comes, she cannot die.

I found it hard to share words with a friend who was bedridden. I bought him a book as a gift and wrote on the front page so when he was by himself he could read, *Our sorrow consists not in the shortness of life, but in our inability to make supreme use of the present moment.* He then could reflect on what this message means for him in his life.

So what does this mean for you and your life? It's a beautiful spring day, and your heart is beating. You're not bedridden; you're able to walk. Yes, you're very fortunate to be in good health, so why not learn to enjoy your life? That's a good question, how can we make ourselves enjoy life?

Without the experience of sadness, frustration, arguments, unhappiness, we would never be able to realize what enlightenment means. Unpleasant, unhappy happenings in your life are important opportunities to experience, to learn from, and then to grow. So please don't be disgusted with yourself, nor get disgusted by your friends, your society, your community, your nation or even other nations. This is the place where we are able to experience life and the joy of enlightenment.

What I am saying about looking at death, accepting death as a reality, is not a negative way of looking at things. When we truly know the meaning of death and dying, we are able to see the meaning of living. To know dying is to know living. We usually think we will live a certain amount of time beyond where we are living now. I am fifty, so I might have thirty years left, and if I live that long, I'll be glad.

But, inhalation and exhalation are a matter of birth and death. If your breath doesn't return to you, you are dead. We're actually living a new life everyday. Buddha Dharma emphasizes you are reborn every day. When you wake up in the morning, place your hands on your heart and say *Wow! My heart is beating this morning! Now what can I do this morning?* Live each day, each new life, live today!

Some priests in training were practicing dana. In this practice, the people share and the priests receive. Each monk knocks on the door of houses and receives whatever is given. When returning home at the conclusion of this practice, the monks would walk in single file after their teachers. It began raining. The teacher, knowing the practitioners wanted to rush to get out of the rain, intentionally walked slowly. One practitioner couldn't stand it and said to the teacher, "Shall we walk a little faster?" The Master said, "If you want to rush, please go ahead."

We have to build up enough spirituality to be able to go ahead.

CATCHING UP

Student: How do you stay centered with everything changing so fast? I can't keep up. I can't stay centered.

Sensei: I understand what you are talking about. People often get caught up in trying to "catch up."

Once you were five years old, now you are twenty-five. You have changed, haven't you? We think we slowly change. But actually we change from minute to minute, so fast. Your girlfriend may say, "I can't catch up with you." Or you may think, "I'm behind in my work. I have to catch up."

Sometimes we consciously or unconsciously expect something to remain constant. We grab at it as a fixed something. But things are changing. We are each changing and becoming. It's helpful to realize what is, and then go along with this realization. Now spring has come and we are moving into summer. We realize it is hot today. Last winter we were cold and we got excited about a snow storm. Now we forget about the snow. Things are changing, becoming, moving on. Interesting, isn't it?

Reality is changing from moment to moment, whether I have the burden of *catching up* or not. If I try to grasp something which I think won't change, then I set up a gap between myself and reality. I think this is an important point. Rather *realize everything changes.*

The consciousness or mentality that I have to catch up, that I am behind, creates frustrations, questions, a heavy burden of pressure. I feel behind sometimes, but usually I don't create such frustrations.

So here we are. Consciously let the past go. You are here in the Cleveland Buddhist Temple. Absolutely stay. If someone else rushes you, tell them, "Please go ahead." I recall a story of some priests in training, practicing dana. In this practice, the people share and the priests receive. Each monk knocks on the door of houses and receives whatever is given. When returning home at the conclusion of this practice, the monks would walk single file after their teacher. It began raining. The teacher, knowing the practitioners wanted to rush to get out of the rain, intentionally walked slowly. One practitioner couldn't stand it and said to the teacher, "Shall we walk a little faster?" The Master said, "If you want to rush, please go ahead."

We have to build up enough spirituality to be able to go ahead. So put your whole self into sitting or meditating, walking and chanting this evening.

As long as you talk about the love of God, you are outside the love of God. The person who is living in the love of God doesn't talk about it. So enjoy your life.

ENLIGHTENMENT

All of you students coming to Tuesday and Wednesday evenings, do not lose your wish and hope to become enlightened. Whether you become enlightened or not is secondary. But having such a hope and wish will create such energy. This energy will make you enlightened. It does!

Also, it is important to puzzle *What is enlightenment?* Keep it as your question. Hold it, but don't be too serious. Keep it in the corner of your mind. Remember I said, "There is no such thing as what we conceptualize as *enlightenment.*" So don't analyze it. Someday it will make sense to you.

Don't misunderstand me. I'm the same as you are. I don't know much. We usually try to know more and more. I am the same way. So what about *enlightenment?* The leaves on the trees are changing to more and more brilliant colors. Horses have four legs. Chickens have two. My life is filled with appreciations.

Student: What is enlightenment?
Sensei: Very Good!

Oh -- was that a question? Well, if that's an answer, you are perfect. That's enlightenment. *What is enlightenment?* is a great answer.

If that was a question, please do not lose your curiosity and keep walking. Maybe five or ten years from now you'll see. You'll think, "Oh, yeh. Some guy at the Cleveland Buddhist Temple told me my asking the question *What is enlightenment?* was enlightenment!"

Suppose I said, "If you come to this temple ten more times, you will reach enlightenment." But I can't guarantee such a thing. I don't say, "I'll guarantee it!" very often. One thing I can guarantee is that each one of us will die. I think we should realize this, instead of being hung up on *I believe this or that. I believe Buddha is the one. I believe Jesus Christ is my savior.* These beliefs are fine. But we need to encourage ourselves to open our eyes of wisdom.

Gee. I am. I am living today and dying today. I may die tonight even. I may disappear from this world of human beings. So I can guarantee that I will die and that each of you will die.

No doubt it is raining outside right now. Realize this fact of life. Maybe you should walk for five blocks in the rain instead of meditating and listening to my talk. Words, words, words! I think the word *Love.* This is very different from moments when I shake Sam's hand or when I share a meal with Mary and we laugh together. In moments like these I feel much more than when I conceptualize *love.* We can always talk about what rain is like, what love is like or what enlightenment is like. But remember, walking in the rain is very different from talking about it. People truly know rain when they are walking in rain and feeling it strike their faces. Most of the time, people who are actually experiencing it hardly put it in words. But they feel such joy inside.

I also guarantee that there is no so-called thing which we conceptualize and call *enlightenment.* About the time you become so-called enlightened, then you are walking in enlightenment. In this case, you appreciate and enjoy your life. Whatever you experience has impact and you always learn from it. Thus, joy of life arises.

Did I make you confused? If so, now you can enjoy the confusion. It is a creative confusion.

The master saw such openness, saw Dozen giving himself, throwing himself open in a spiritual sense. The master grabbed that chance. The master said, "Oh, you are dumb again! You ask such questions." In his mind the master thought, "Hey! What honesty! What emptiness!" Emptiness is the key. The master did not say any of this. Rather, with energies, expressing with his eyes, the master communicated with Dozen. This shocked Dozen and Dozen realized it. Dozen was enlightened. Dozen gasshoed with such a smile and left the Dokusan.

WHERE DID YOU COME FROM?

Dozen visited a well-known Chinese Zen master. Dozen was to become a great Zen master himself one day, but at the time of this story Dozen was a student.

During Dokusan, a private interview with the master, the master asked Dozen, "Where did you come from?"

So I ask you, "Where did you come from?"

Our common way to answer this question is "West 152nd and Detroit," or "Lorain," or "South Euclid" or some other geographical location. If you are stopped by a policeman and he says, "Let me see your driver's license. Where do you live?" it's expected that you answer him with the geographical place in which you live.

But when you come here, you are not looking for common conversation as you use in your daily life. Also, I am not here right now to share common conversation with you. We have enough of such exchanges throughout our daily lives. The master asked Dozen from a spiritual level the question *Where did you come from?* In the same way I am asking you this question from a spiritual level. When I tell you this, you attempt to think deeper. You may think, *What does the Bible say?* Or *What do the Buddhist Sutras say?* Or *What did I read?* You reflect on ideas from our religious training. You might think *Well, Christians believe . . . Jews believe . . . Buddhists are aware of . . .* You may think the answers you come up with in this manner are *deeper* than saying, "I'm from South Euclid."

Go beyond titles and names, beyond knowledge, beyond beliefs, philosophy and logic. Then what do you answer when the teacher asks, "Where did you come from?"

Craig: From the void. From nowhere.

Sensei: It still smells of knowledge which you have gained. *Where do you come from?* You could say *I am sitting here in this chair* or *Spring has come."*

People listening may think, "He is stupid. He's not answering the question." It doesn't matter where a person comes from, if he or she truly testifies to the absoluteness of the existence of his or her life. It doesn't matter whether they are a single parent or not, whether they are black, white, or yellow. But, so it is! So here I am. Such an answer comes out from yourself.

If you truly realize the truthfulness of the existence of your life, the answer you give to such questions will always be the same. The words you use may be different, the energy somewhat different, but the answer will be the same.

Most of the time we give one answer as Craig did when he said, "The void." Then we think, "That's not a good answer. I'll have to think of something different, something better." Often we have the consciousness to impress others. Or we might understand that it is a Zen question, so may say nothing.

Dozen was not enlightened at the time of the Zen story which I am about to tell you. When the Zen master asked Dozen, "Where did you come from?" Dozen gave a geographical name, a common sense answer.

The master with patience and compassion asked the question a second time in a slightly different way, "What were you doing this summer?"

Dozen responded, "I was attending summer sesshin at such and such a place."

The master thought in his mind, "Realize it, see it, read my mind. I'm not expecting such an answer." But the master said, "When did you leave the summer sesshin?"

Dozen responded, "September 25" or some other date.

The master said vehemently, "How dumb you are! You are not worthy to be hit even. Hitting you is a waste of my time!" The master rang the bell and Dozen left.

Dozen was much experienced at Zen practice, in contrast with other students. As he left the private interview, he was extremely disappointed. He thought, "He didn't even hit me. He said the interview was a waste of his time!"

Dozen didn't sleep that night. First thing in the morning he went back to Dokusan or a private interview with the master again. Dozen bowed and threw himself spiritually into the master.

Dozen said, "I didn't understand. I honestly answered you when you questioned me. But you said hitting me is a waste of your time. Please teach me. What was wrong?"

The master saw such openness, saw Dozen giving himself, throwing himself open in a spiritual sense. The master grabbed that chance. The master said, "Oh, you are dumb again! You ask such questions." In his mind the master thought, "Hey! What honesty! What emptiness!" Emptiness is the key. The master did not say any of this. Rather, with energies, expressing with his eyes, the master communicated with Dozen. This shocked Dozen and Dozen realized it. Dozen was enlightened in the master's compassionate silence. Dozen gasshoed with such a smile and left the Dokusan.

So the question *Where did you come from?* was very simple. But the Zen master was not talking from a common sense level in which we all know the place where we come from. Rather he expected Dozen to exchange with him in a heart-to-heart manner. At this level you have to be real.

So when you truly open yourself spiritually, then things come into you and become yours. But most of the time our minds are filled with knowledge, conceptions and past experiences which we carry around with us. We cannot help ourselves. We judge situations from such knowledge, conceptions, and past experiences. We think *good, bad, right, wrong, yea, nay, It makes sense.* This kind of thing.

Because of this it takes enormous time for many people to realize what I am talking about. I have some students who stayed with me for five or six years and yet they don't realize this. Someone else walks in with such emptiness and realizes the essence of what Dharma is teaching us. Interesting, isn't it? It's great.

So what is there to realize? Peonies bloom on peony trees. A cat doesn't become a chicken. Tulips are tulips, not roses. Why can't we realize this true fact? That to be me is great. I don't have to be anyone but me. I am blooming as I am in my life, just as a peony blooms on a peony tree. Further, a beautiful peony flower does not worry about when it will wilt and fall to the ground. It does not compete with the flower next to it; rather it blooms with its whole self.

So what am I like since I realize this? I'll give you one answer, but keep looking and searching for there are many answers.

I was recently at a memorial service in New York City. A man asked me, "Don't you become nervous sitting with clergy people of other religions and consul generals, dignitaries and ambassadors from Japan?"

I responded, "Yes, I have a consciousness that they have such titles and names. But, strangely enough, I don't get nervous from that type of idea, because the ambassador cannot be me. I am the one who is truly living my life."

My life cannot be some other person's life. This does not mean I try to be an egoistic person. I just greet people, I say "Hi!"

This man continued to ask me questions after I gave the Dharma talk, "Don't you think you forgot something in your Dharma talk?"

I said, "Yes, I do. But it's over. It's done. What can I do? I'm always able to learn from any situation and condition. I love myself the most, so I can learn to take care of myself from the experience and I'll do better the next chance I get."

I'm not talking about considering your life or aspects of your life as good or bad, right or wrong. We spend so much time and energy making judgements. I do this too. We think, "This is good. That's bad." We consider what others will think. "No one is looking at me so I'll do this." Or "No one noticed how hard I worked!"

So where did you come from? What I am talking about is spiritual awareness. Instead of making judgements, sincerely realize or awaken yourself that your life is absolute. Exist at the absolute place here and now.

*What kind of questions we have, also
the vows and the wishes we have, are
the ways we build up our lives.*

ENJOY THE COOL ONE

I am glad to see you before we each become senile. About two weeks ago my wife and I visited an old age home. Being in the old age home brings me a sense to develop kindness, compassion or skills which will help to live my life in a meaningful way. In a deep sense, can I enjoy my life while I am in good health? Are you enjoying your life?

I go to the old age home to visit Soyu Matsuoka Roshi. When he sees me he puts his palms together in gassho and says, "Thank you, thank you." After a moment he says, "Who are you?"

He has a picture of a movie actress on the wall instead of a picture of Buddha. I remembered that my father used to say, "Instead of giving 100 words, it is better to give a massage," so I started to give him a shiatsu massage. He said to me, "Maybe your wife is better at giving a massage."

I also have such a consciousness to enjoy the differences between a male and female touch. I stepped back and my wife gave Roshi a massage.

He said, "This is much better. Thank you. Thank you." He enjoyed, and he doesn't remember who we are.

While our consciousness is clear or under control, why not assist ourselves and others to enjoy life? What does enjoyment mean? We generally think we enjoy such occasions as a delicious meal with drinks. When asked about enjoyment, a man generally thinks of enjoying time with a woman, and a woman enjoys time with a man, or a man with a man, or a woman with a woman. But when we eat or drink too much, we suffer. Interesting, isn't it?

One of my teachers kept saying over and over to me, "Are you enjoying *it*?" I thought he was dumb in always asking this question without saying what *it* was. When I was growing up, I had a close, caring relationship with my grandmother. When she died, the teacher intentionally came to me and asked me, "Are you enjoying it?"

I said, "I'm sad. I'm not enjoying it."

He smiled gently and said, "Sad, yes. And yet, Are you enjoying *it*?"

I can still hear his voice.

Why can't we enjoy it? is a good question.

On a cool day in fall I was on the elevator coming down from the fourth floor of the Holiday Inn. A man on the elevator with me said, "It's time summer has come to an end."

I said, "Yes, time does not wait for us."

He said, "Yes!"

Isn't that beautiful? I shared such simple words with a stranger. Actually we are not strangers. I just say that because we haven't talked before in my memory.

Here in America, people exchange beautiful expressions: *Enjoy the day! Enjoy the sunshine! Have a good time!*

As I was busily packing at home, my twelve year old daughter said to me, "Have a nice trip!"

We tend to ignore or see these expressions as just gestures. When I empty myself, which means simply be myself, and someone says to me, "Have a nice trip," I feel Wow! Thank you!

Instead of having this kind of awareness, we normally create frustration. We think such things as, "I have to do this and he doesn't!" or "I took care of my child for seventeen years and she still doesn't respect or listen to me!" Or we may think, "I have a problem with my boss." All of these thoughts relate to what we judge as right or wrong, convenient or inconvenient, beneficial or not beneficial to us. In this way we put distance between our circumstances and ourselves. Instead we can think, "That's my life."

Right now I may put myself *into* talking; you may put yourself *into* listening. When I say this, it seems like I'm making an effort to put myself *into* it. But for real things one doesn't have to make an effort.

Most of the time we ignore this way of being and we look for something joyful. We think, "I can't have joy in Cleveland, maybe in California, maybe in Japan or India." Or we think such things as, "I'll never be happy because of *him*." You don't have to look for real joy.

We have recited many times:
Form is no other than Sunyata. Sunyata is no other than form. Then the Heart Sutra says No . . . No . . No . . . No attainment!

Form is no other than Sunyata, has to do with being in the here and now. Many give this advice, but it is not always easy to be *in it.* I will make the mistake of trying to intellectually explain the second part, *Sunyata is no other than form.* Later maybe you will realize it. This is not my business; it is your business.

Sunyata is no other than form. We each have all kinds of experiences in our lives. We have this when we feel stupid, when we feel great, frustrated, discouraged, happy, recognized, not recognized. We all have such experiences as we live in our social structure. Prior to your life you had Sunyata consciousness. Sunyata can be translated as emptiness or Suchness or Is-ness. Sunyata consciousness eliminates my judgements of good and bad, right and wrong, beneficial and not beneficial. That we have the relationships we have is a true fact of our lives. There is another way of saying this. I may like you or I may not like you. This does not matter. Either way it is amazing enough that we know each other and share moments together.

Another way I intellectually think about the meaning of the phrase *Sunyata is no other than form* has to do with a *cool one*. This cool one (not necessarily a calm one) has no name, no color, no form. This *cool one* sees when you are frustrated, when you cry, when you are exuberant. Each one of you is living with a *cool guy or gal* looking at you. When you are frustrated you can have a conversation with this *cool one*. A more ordinary approach to this is to think that everything in my life is a gift and I can learn from it. With this way of learning, spiritual energy will grow.

It is easy for me to say this; whether I can do this or not is another question. I smile at myself a lot. When you smile at yourself, you are already *in it*. This is very different from consciously analyzing what I am doing. I have been talking like this and meditating with people like you for thirty-five years. Why do I have to meditate so many times? I'd rather lie down on the couch.

*I found myself rushing to a funeral
service. Then I thought, "The service
can't start without me! And if I get
frustrated, my talk will be mixed up."
So I told myself, "Calm down."
Try to be the best of yourself whatever
you do. We are so busy, busy. We rush
around. But, "Where are we going?"
is a good question.*

AN IRON BALL IN YOUR MOUTH

Is anyone here for the first time? Nice to see you. In this case "nice" means something beyond good and bad, right and wrong. In order to meet each other, we live in this certain time period and in this certain space. Also, you didn't have to come and here you are. We all look for some kind of miracle, for something grand to happen, for a savior to come from someplace to save us. But I say, *this* is enough, this is miracle enough. I am here. You are here. Your heart is beating. Whether my talk is judged as good or bad, you are able to hear it and I am talking. Isn't that amazing?

We all put energy into communicating with each other. Truly communicating with each other is almost impossible, but we think it is possible. Do you know why it is close to impossible? It is because you are changing and I am changing. Things are changing, becoming and moving on. In this changing world we are continually having new thoughts, new feelings. Yet we are here to communicate in these seconds. It's almost impossible. We speak of the difficulty of Russians and Americans meeting each other in space. Yet communication between us has similar difficulties. We think we understand what we hear others say to us. But do we really understand their meaning? Do you think at some moments there is perfect communication between you and your spouse, or between you and your friends? If so, then you can get excited about what a fantastic thing this is; this is miracle enough.

So usually we mis-communicate with others and misinterpret others' words and actions, but we think we understand each other. The rush-rush of our modern world increases this tendency. The so-called smart people created such a world! Modern technology has brought us cellular phones, computers and fax machines, food prepared instantly and much more. So our life can get easier, more comfortable, more convenient, and so it is. But we get so frustrated and are under such pressure. I am teaching a meditation class in the evening for a small college in Chicago. The administrator of the school called me and said, "We already have thirty people signed up and it is way before the deadline for enrollment. How many can you teach in this class?" This showed me people are living in such pressure and many are looking for some way to comfort themselves and to have a peaceful mind.

We live with so many smart people, with so much education, with modern technology which makes things go faster and faster and become more and more convenient. Yet we live under such pressure. Is this ridiculous?

We may be driven crazy living with this modern technology without finding peacefulness in our minds. So here are the senior leaders of Zen Shin Sangha. They are kind enough to come here to prepare the temple for my

Dharma talk and our sitting meditation. This encourages each of us to go back to our original nature of each one's life. Can you *Drop it!*? Can you drop what is in your mind? Or does your mind go on and on and on?

I was walking down Michigan Avenue in Chicago talking with my friend. We stopped to look at a map. A woman approached us and said, "Can I help? Can I give you some directions?"

I smiled and thought, "What a beautiful person we have in Chicago!" I told her where we wished to go.

She smiled and said, "You speak English! " She gave me the needed directions and we began talking.

I told her I am a so-called Buddhist priest, a minister at the Midwest Buddhist Temple. I said, "It is my great pleasure to see a person like you extending help in this busy life. Most people have no time or just don't seem to care."

She smiled and responded, "I have a lunch break."

Isn't that beautiful? While I was talking with her, another lady walked behind us. She was screeching. I cannot copy her words exactly. "Yaak, Yaak!" We were startled and looked at her. I was quiet. I smiled at her. The lady on the lunch break told me, "I like to scream sometimes like she is," and smiled. Most of us would have judged the screaming lady as mentally ill. I don't have to scream, but sometimes I feel like screaming on the streets too. So the woman on the lunch break and I could understand this screaming woman.

Whatever we dream, whatever we may normally do, when conditions change we don't know what we might do. Am I discouraging you? I am talking from the very bottom line of spiritual awareness. So if you live in our modern world and have never walked down the street screaming, then you are very fortunate. If this is so for you, are you grateful?

I have been training myself, studying and practicing for years and years. But all this can disappear in a crisis of emotional explosions. So I love myself. I never get tired of myself even though I get tired of you sometimes and you get tired of me.

Have you experienced a crisis of emotional explosions? What can you do then? Spiritual practice is like holding a large, burning iron ball in your mouth. Whoa! Whoa! It is too hot to swallow. You cannot swallow it; you cannot spit it out. If you swallow it, you will burn yourself. If you spit it out, you quit seeking, searching for the meaning of life.

Then how do I live? Carelessly? Full of acquisitions? Do I do anything I feel like? *What shall I do?* is a good question.

Remember *this*. Hold *it*. Then you have the iron ball in your mouth. You cannot swallow it, nor spit it out. Then someday, some awareness will come through. Then smile at yourself. When you smile, you taste it. Then you smile at how the experience is like having an iron ball in your mouth.

So we will practice sitting; it will help us to settle ourselves.

Five

What about living with other people?

" It is inconceivable, Yen relationship;
it is indeed unexplainable "

Yen means a relationship with all beings.

We each have freedom to like certain people and to dislike others. Yet we practice respect for each one's truthfulness of life. Gassho is a gesture to show respect to each others' truthfulness. Of course, you do not have to bow or gassho in public for people may think you are strange! But do practice respect for each one's life in this way. Some of us may call ourselves Buddhist; others of us may have a strong belief in Jesus as the only Savior; others may have great price in their Jewish heritage. Here we practice respecting each one's truthfulness of life whether our beliefs coincide with theirs or not.

LIFE IS STRICTLY RESPECTED!

We all live with hypocrisy, especially religious hypocrisy. We think to ourselves, "Love thy neighbor." Yes, to be a good Christian or a good Buddhist or a good Jew, we do need to make an effort to love our neighbors. Yes, this effort is better than putting a lot of energy into hating our neighbors. It's beautiful, even.

As human beings, we cannot deny our emotional reactions. We have feelings of likes and dislikes. There are some people with whom we prefer to associate. There are people of whom we are not fond. So how can we love *all* our neighbors and not be hypocritical? After all, there *are* people we frankly do not like.

I think, from a certain kind of awareness and compassion, we become friendly with others effortlessly. In order to gain some level of understanding of this awareness, let's truly realize we are each born with an interesting nature. After our birth we become so wise and smart -- so proud of our cultural and racial heritage, that our nature gets covered up. Many people dislike, even hate, people who are different from themselves, particularly people with a cultural and religious background different from their own.

In order to see that we are each born with a unique nature, go back to the time of our birth. When we were born, we each were naked. May we truly realize it. Our energies were expressed with the cry, "Yah!" We didn't tell ourselves such things as *I can't yell loudly because my father is an alcoholic* or *I can't yell because my mother is a single parent.* At the time of your birth you have no such consciousness. Your voice comes out through you, with you. You didn't try to yell. You just yelled.

Zazen meditation practice can help us get in touch with this nature with which we were born. This was our nature before we were instilled with thoughts from our family, friends and culture. We don't have to express this with words. But feelings can be practiced with our hearts. So our words, eyes, actions from our bodies are so extended to others.

We can generate this kind of awareness even for people we initially do not like. How do I create this awareness within myself? With this awareness, first, I frankly admit to myself *I am not fond of this person. I don't like this person. Yet he is living his life. He has one life to live, just as I do. He is dying or getting closer to his death every minute, just as I am. The cause of his death is his birth, just as the cause of my death is my birth. Sooner or later he will be old and die. Or he may die without old age. He could have a heart attack tomorrow. Right now he is living his life. Sooner or later he will disappear from this world, and so will I.* I keep this awareness within myself. Through reflecting on this practice, I expand sympathy and love. This could be called a compassionate heart.

Now I don't say to this person, "You'll die sooner or later." But by channeling my thoughts in this way, it is easier to say, "Hi."

People ask me if I experience racial discrimination as I live here in America. No, I answer. I have lived here thirty years and I have never felt racial discrimination. When people approach me with this kind of mentality, I don't react to it. For a few minutes I change my energies. I transform or soothe them. Most of the time I end up with a friend.

One night I was coming out of a bar and a lady who was drunk was sitting on the floor. She looked at me and said, "I cannot stand Chinese."

I paused, smiled and said, "I know that you are sitting there. Are you alright?"

She laughed.

When someone says or does something hurtful or mean, we usually react with similar energies. We usually say to ourselves or to our friends *He is mean* or *He is nasty.* Instead, I examine my emotions, see if similar emotions exist in my mind. Then I get rid of them, at least for a short moment, and associate with the person. By examining and soothing my emotions, I often turn a person who treats me meanly into someone who is friendly.

Sometimes we are afraid someone will not like us or will not give us what we want. Through our practice we can work with our energies in these situations also. Someone recently said to me, "I have an interview tomorrow for a job I really want. I don't know if I will say the right things or not." I say to this person, "Forget about it! Don't assume, guess, worry about what questions they might ask. *Drop it!* Be simply as you are. If they don't like you, they won't hire you. So apply other places."

Whether we like or dislike each other, there is no doubt we can learn to respect each other's lives. Life itself is beyond our cheap judgements of likes and dislikes, good and bad, or right and wrong. This practice helps us to respect each other's lives through the realization of the truthfulness of our lives. We can respect each other's lives without hypocrisy. Life itself, before we judge good and bad or right and wrong, is strictly respected.

Why are you like you are? Why do you like one person and not another? I don't know. But so we are. There is no one exactly the same as you. Even twins are different. Each of us has a life to live and each has a different nature. Fantastic, isn't it? *Oneness is indeed a recognition of difference.*

On the golf course people use more
holy words than they use in church.
For example, when my golf buddy hits
the ball askew, he says, "Jesus Christ!"
and he hits the ground with his club.
This friend has taught me many such
expressions on the golf course.   He
came twice to the beginner's meditation
classes.   Then he quit coming. He said,
"What is this? What the heck!" But he
is a sharp person.   He was born with
such a nature to grab what he needs
right there when he needs it.

A TEACHER, FRIENDS AND NOURISHING YOUR LIFE

My golf buddy called me up this morning to see if we could play golf together, but my schedule didn't allow it. His voice was somewhat depressed so I asked him, "How are you?"

He's an honest person, aware of this feelings. He said, "I'm depressed and unhappy. Give me some words of wisdom."

I said, "Maybe you should forget about what is happiness and unhappiness. Then you can be truly yourself. Possibly less depressed then."

Then he said after a short silence, "That makes sense."

I said, "It makes sense to me, too."

He said, "My, my, my. I'm lucky I called you up this morning."

Do you see why I say he is a sharp man? He was able to see that this bit of wisdom could help his life along and he thanked me for it.

Generally we say we have *good friends*. But I say it is important to have friends who do not try to dominate us, but rather who share wisdom. Such friends do not pretend to admire us. Rather they tell us the truth as they see it. They share wisdom. Wisdom is cool, yet precise, direct and simple.

A large number of people call me on the telephone and say such things as, "I read a book on Zen meditation and I want to learn it," or "I'm impressed with Buddhist teaching and I want to learn more about it." Many of these people talk a lot, read a lot and plan a lot, but they never come to practice. Talking, planning, thinking, knowing are completely different from doing. This is particularly true in religious practice. So you came here. Such action is important. Buddhist wisdom says it is a waste of energy to argue about beliefs. "I am a Jew. Jews believe this, Catholics believe that . . . and on and on." I identify myself as a Buddhist, but so what? I'm simply a human being, simply living my life.

Some people simply live. They don't argue about what they believe. It is easy to ignore such people, but these are the people who will share wisdom. *It's important to honor and get acquainted with a teacher and friends who share wisdom and teachings which nourish.* How you nourish your thinking can make a big difference in your life. Such a teacher and friends will definitely help your life along!

A woman had an errant son. She asked her brother, a Zen priest, to talk with him and "straighten him out," so to speak. The Zen master spent time with the sister and her son but did not speak to the son about his errant ways. Yet the son changed his ways drastically. How can this be?

SHOW ME WHERE THERE IS NO HOT OR COLD

A student asked a Zen master, "How can I find the place where there is no hot and no cold?"

The Zen master said, "When it is hot, die in the hotness. When it is cold, die in the coldness."

Here is a clue I will give you for this koan: In this case hot and cold means more than Fahrenheit and centigrade, it means more than just temperature. I want to tell you a story which to me is related to this koan.

The sister of a Zen priest called her brother. She was very distraught because her son had become wayward. He spent his time with sex, drugs and that culture's version of rock and roll. She asked her brother, the priest, to come to visit her home and to do something about her son. The priest came to visit his sister's house. The first day he appreciated his sister's hospitality for he was used to the austerity of the Zen monastery. But he said nothing to the son. The second day he still did not talk to the son about his errant ways. By the third day, the sister began complaining to the priest that he was not talking to her son. She expected her brother, the priest, to sit her son down and lecture him, but the priest never did this. He only observed the son coming and going from the house. On the fourth day, the Zen master prepared to leave to go back to his monastery. He asked the errant son to tie his sandals. As the son did so, a tear came from the priest's eye and fell on the son's hand. Still the Zen priest did not say a word to the son about how the son was spending his time and energy. He bade good-bye to his sister and her son. To his sister's amazement after the Zen priest's visit, the son changed his ways and began putting his time and energy into productive pursuits.

So what brought about this change? How did the Zen priest's actions impact the son so greatly? He did not even talk with the son!

Many teachers would just tell this story, but not explain it. It is my karma to make attempts at explaining stories like this one.

The Zen priest truly felt the anguish and frustration of the son; he truly felt the same as the son. *When we are one with our own anguish, we can truly feel others' pain. This empathy may impact their life.*

So when you are hot, be hot, die in the hotness. When you are cold, be cold, die in the coldness. If you fall and hurt your knee, embrace the pain in your knee. Most of the time we think that someone who has terminal cancer would hate the cancer. But by hating the cancer, one is hating life itself. The Zen master thoroughly understood this.

We usually separate ourselves by trying to be happy and hating our misery. Don't worry about the conceptualized idea of happy and unhappy. If someone says to you, "You seem to be happy," say, "Thank you." Or even if they say, "You seem so unhappy," say, "Yes, I am miserable." Neither is good or bad, but both are life itself. When we separate ourselves from happiness and unhappiness, we separate from life itself. When we are with someone who understands this, we feel very comfortable. That's the way we learn from any happenings in life. In this way we enrich our lives in wholeness.

When it is cold, be cold. When it is hot, be hot. Do not create more than the cold and hot that exists.

It is said that at his birth, Shakyamuni Buddha took seven steps and, pointing to the sky and to the earth, proclaimed, "I alone am the most honored one above the heaven and below the earth." We know it is impossible for a newborn baby to do such thing But what is the meaning of this story for us?

See your life itself, beyond such artificial categories as name, race, gender, and social class. Take these heavy things off and move into the lightness of springtime. Then you realize that your own life exists uniquely in the universe.

IT'S NEVER TOO LATE!

Two days before I moved from Cleveland to Chicago, a retired Nisei, second generation Japanese American, visited me to extend his farewell to me. He said, "I came to thank you and to apologize because I could not help you out as much as I should have in expanding the Buddha Dharma to non-Buddhist people in this area." He continued, "I understood in my head that I should not discriminate against people by their color, yet I could not deny my uncomfortable feeling deep inside. That feeling was not only toward the white and black race, but even for Japanese people from Japan." He smiled knowing that I was from Japan.

Then he continued, "Once, when I was a young boy, I was waiting for my turn at a barber shop. The barber shouted, 'Hey, Boy! I do not cut Japs' hair! Go home and ask your Papa-san to cut your hair.' I was astonished and embarrassed in front of people." Even though fifty years had passed since this incident had happened, humiliation showed on his face.

After keeping quiet for a short moment, he related, "One year later the evacuation of Japanese Americans occurred. We were told to move out from our house with two suitcases. We were taken to a horse race track." He continued, "We stayed in remodeled horse stalls. Oh, it really smelled of horse shit."

After a few months, he was put on a train and did not know the destination. "All the windows were blanked out and soldiers guarded us with guns. I thought we would be shot to death at some unknown place." His face showed fear, but he smiled and said, "Well, I will quit talking like this."

Changing the subject he said, "You have been working to propagate the Buddha Dharma among the different races in this conservative area for fifteen years. Now I give you credit and respect for this work you have done. To be honest, during the first few years I was hoping you would get discouraged and leave. But you did not, so I quit coming to your services. Then I started worrying the hakujin, the white race, might take over the temple. When a hakujin became the President of the temple, I thought *That's it. I spread the word Komatta bon-san ga kitayo, a troublesome priest has come. He is making a big mistake and creating trouble.* I gave you a hard time, but you did not quit. Later I realized that these hakujin, who were coming to the temple were sincere. When one of the hakujin thanked me for welcoming him to the temple, I was embarrassed and ashamed of myself. He was a more sincere Buddhist than I was. I was a Buddhist by habit. You know, Sensei, I generally thought I should be a member of the temple because some day I have to ask the temple to assist at my funeral service. I also felt I should be a member for the sake of my ancestry and my parents." Then he hesitated, "I don't know enough about Buddhist teachings to be a confident Buddhist. I often do not identify myself as a Buddhist because I do not want my friends to ask me about Buddhist teachings.

"Well, Sensei, I still cannot deny the discomfort of being with hakujin, the white race. Yet I cannot deny my respect for their sincerity in seeking the meaning of life from Buddhist teachings. I really give you credit and respect, Sensei." The Nisei said further, "Sensei, you know my son and daughter are both married to hakujins with the Christian faith. Now-a-days, this young generation choose their mates because of beauty and often they do not choose mates with the same racial heritage. Just as you say, Sensei, time passes and things are changing, moving and becoming -- this is a basic teaching of Buddha Dharma, the so-called Law of Impermanence, isn't it? I became aware of this Dharma, the truth."

I thought in my mind, "Hey! Not too late for this Nisei to realize the Dharma."

The Nisei continued, "I hope my grandchildren go to Dharma School. I really hope the temple will welcome interracial children and interfaith children."

I agreed and in my mind I thought, "Hey! Now he is singing a different tune. The shoe is on the other foot." I didn't say this. Rather, we talked about how we should be prepared and ready with attractive programs for the new generation -- for anyone who is seeking the meaning of life from Buddha Dharma.

We already know what we should do, what we could do. It is time to do it. Let's take action. Let's do it before people are truly tired. Is it too late? *It is never too late.*

Most of the time we see from our self-consciousness and we see happenings in our life as a fixed concept. Please do not conclude anything about what is happening. I think being a conclusion seeker is a modern sickness. Some teenagers actually kill themselves because they arrive at a conclusion about their lives. We need to keep in mind that beyond these conclusions in our minds, there is a purpose of becoming. Things are changing, becoming and moving on. We are living in the process of becoming and changing and moving on.

GRATITUDE TOWARD OUR PARENTS

This switch is on now. Is your switch on? That's a good question, isn't it? It is not my responsibility. We each have much freedom to turn our switches on or off.

Most children do not have their switches on when their mom and dad talk. They're smart, though. They pretend that they are listening, but nothing comes into their receiver.

I am going to talk about gratitude toward parents, particularly mothers. Either because of modern mentality or Western mentality, we do not talk much about gratitude toward mothers and fathers. In a sutra written 2500 years ago, Shakyamuni Buddha spoke about feeling gratitude for parents. The Sutra is called *The Heart of Gratitude for Father and Mother*. This sutra especially emphasizes mothers. A baby stays in her mother's womb for nine months. Also in olden times men would go out hunting for food to feed the families, but the mother stayed home caring for the babies. For this reason the mother is very much emphasized in this Sutra.

First, there is the gratitude to your mother for holding and protecting you with her body for nine months. Your mother shared her flesh and blood with you. Because of this you received your body.

Second, there is the gratitude to your mother for giving birth to you. When the time came for your birth, your mother felt acute, searing pain in her whole body. Sometimes a mother exchanges her life for the new life of her baby. How many of you can think about exchanging your life for someone else to live? When a mother hears the voice of her baby being born, she feels she is being reborn at the same time. Your mother felt like she was being reborn when you were born. Isn't that amazing?

I will put the third, fourth and fifth gratitude together. There is the gratitude for being nurtured and nursed. Though a woman likes to look attractive, a mother does not care about losing her shapely figure and she will nurse her baby to keep her baby healthy. Also a mother nursing her baby does not sleep through the night for she is awakened by the baby's cry so that she can feed and diaper her baby. A mother does not hesitate to clean up the dirty bottom of her baby. Have you ever seen a mother lift up the baby's stuff and say, "Wow! That's a healthy one." There is also the gratitude to your mother for tasting the sweet and bitter food before she gave it to you, her baby. Or for tasting to see if the baby's food is too hot or too cold or poison or not.

The Sutra says that mothers will even consciously create bad karma for themselves to help their children. A story in Buddhist mythology tells of a disciple of Shakyamuni Buddha using his super powers to see a mother in hell. This mother was in hell because in life she had been so poor that she had stolen food to feed her son, who later became a well-known disciple of Buddha.

We also can be aware of the gratitude for our mothers thinking about our safety. A mother thinks about her child day and night, hoping her child is safe, as long as she is alive. Even after she dies, she wishes to guide and protect her child.

All this was written 2500 years ago. It's interesting today, isn't it?

Anything you would like to say?

Jeff: Here is a young student visiting us. Can you tell us what is the essence of Buddhism?

Sensei: I have been a so-called Buddhist minister for thirty-three years and I am still learning. That's the Buddhist way, endlessly learning. What is the Buddhist way? It's Mother's Day. If your mother still survives, even if you do not like her, send her a card. We think about something big and important like enlightenment, wisdom, love, compassion. We hear people say things like, "I've studied with someone from India or Japan or China." We keep attending workshops and seminars. We go to the library and the book store. We find so many books to read to answer a question like, "What is the essence of Buddhism?" Yet we can't even send a card to our mothers. Do you know a person who is truly living in love, caring for another, crying and laughing with them? Such a person doesn't talk about it. She does not ask such questions even. She is *in it;* her life *is* Buddha Dharma.

Dennis: Sensei, what would you say to someone who had been hurt badly by his or her mother or father? Say the person has experienced incest with one parent?

Sensei: I would feel badly for this person. With tears in my eyes I would say to him or her, "So what? What can you learn from this experience?"

Yes, sometimes I may think some of my experiences are hard for me. Yet, I think, "What can I learn from this experience?" This is the attitude of someone seeking the meaning of life. Each experience in my life is a gift, a chance to learn and to advance my life. I try not to ignore any experience, no matter how painful. This is what I would want to convey to such a person.

Even if an experience is hard to bare, we can still ask ourselves *What can I learn from this?* What we have learned is what we get and what we are today.

You may have heard the story of Bodhidharma saying, "There is no merit in virtuous acts." to the emperor who had done extensive great deeds. The emperor was quite disappointed with this answer. What Bodhidharma was talking about relates to being in desperate situations. Yes, we can build up karma with good deeds, but almost always there is self-pride in these actions, the feeling of, "Look what I did!" In contrast, when we become desperate, we have to give up, our spirits fall to the depths. Often it is at such times we can realize the oneness of the immeasurable, unhindered light which brightens in ten directions. We can realize we are living in it.

THE PRIMAL VOW: NAMU AMIDA BUTSU

It is easy to misunderstand Shin Buddhism. To have realizations of Shin, one needs to be spiritually mature. Can you realize that we *are* living in the unhindered light of immeasurable wisdom and compassion? This is quite a realization, isn't it? In order for you to get a feeling of this, I will share a personal experience.

I came to the United States in 1962, when I was twenty years old. I attended a university in Los Angeles extending my training as a Jodoshinshu priest. I had great difficulty with my English. Plus the culture here was vastly different from what I was used to. After I was in this country about a year, I was involved in a car accident. I was unconscious and in the hospital for two days.

After that, I became extremely short-tempered and I had a fight with the head priest. I had to stop going to the university and I was sent back to San Francisco. While in San Francisco, I had a chance to meet with Susuki Roshi, but that is a different story.

After I was in San Francisco for about six months, in a sense I had something like an emotional breakdown. I woke up in a hospital room with about twenty patients. I saw the patients all around me who had trouble related to the brain. Some had bandaged heads, others had difficulty holding a spoon when they ate. Many of them could not talk and others would scream out. I was in the neurology wing of the hospital, but I did not know this then. Actually at that time I did not know the word *neurology* even. I was given a lot of neurological tests.

I could not help myself. I became scared and worried. I thought, "What if I would end up like these people around me?" I felt so alone, so frightened, quite desperate. I thought about calling my family in Japan. But I knew calling them and telling them that I was in the hospital would only worry them. There was nothing they could do for me because they were far across the ocean from San Francisco.

I felt very alone and desolate. I had no friends because I had been in this country for a short time. The only person who came to visit me was a social worker and an executive from the Buddhist Churches of America. I had to sign papers relating to the neurological tests the doctors were giving me. I didn't understand what the papers said, but I signed them anyway.

With such insecurity, uncertainty and feelings of loneliness and desperation, the thought came to me, "What am I doing? I'm a Jodo Jodoshinshu priest." I decided to call the name of Amida Buddha to come to help me. Namu Amida Butsu, Namu Amida Butsu, Namu Amida Butsu. I pulled a cover over my face and recited Amida's name so as not to bother those around me. I also

prayed to Shinto-God to help me. I also have the consciousness
to pray to God." God, please help me. Please help me. Please,
God, help me." I think many people who go to Christian
churches do more or less the same thing.

I did this for several days, but nothing happened. Yes, now
I can laugh. At the time I wasn't laughing. People were
screaming around me. I continued to worry I would be like them.
I thought to myself, "Here I have been praying and invoking
Amida Buddha's name to be helped and I began to feel more
alone and desperate." Also I felt bad because I had lied to the
people when I talked to them about Amida Buddha's Primal Vow
to save all beings, whatever situation they were in.

Then, after about two weeks, I was staring flatly, depressed,
looking at a single flower a nurse had placed on my bed stand.
I saw the flower expanded by light coming out from the flower.
The bright light intensified the red, yellow and green of the single
flower. I was astonished. I was caught in these immeasurable
lights. Then some words arose in my mind. The words were a
poem I had memorized in the past:

Roses are blooming on the rose tree.
There is nothing strange.
The flower blooms silently and falls quietly
        without sound,
Though never again to return to its branch.
Her total existence is expressed in that one place
At that moment.
That is the voice of the flower,
The truth of the single flower on the branch.
Therein lies the joy of life, infinitely radiant and
        everlasting.

These words simply repeated themselves in my mind as I looked at the flower. The light of the flower became brighter and larger. I was taken into this light. Then I realized the immeasurable light and life of Amida Buddha. Namu meant the taking in of me into this light. Namu Amida Butsu meant I and immeasurable life and light are one. I felt the *unhindered light of immeasurable wisdom and compassion.* I realized I had been living in immeasurable compassion and wisdom since I was born.

Tears came to my eyes. I recited Namu Amida Butsu. Then I began to notice how the nurses were working to help me. A nurse had placed the flower on my bed stand. Nurses brought me food. The food had once been living -- chicken, green beans, potatoes. Now they were nourishment for me. Now I realized I had been living in the kindness and sacrifices of others.

I was lucky for one of the nurses was a member of the temple for which I later became a minister. She told me and others after I became her minister, "Reverend Ogui lived in thankfulness even when he was in the neurological wing of the hospital." I told her, "Yes, but not at the beginning of my stay."

It is indeed true that we are living in a great vow of Amida Buddha. This light *is* always shining on us. We *are* living in the life and light of Amida Buddha.

We all wish for a life without regrets. We wish to live in peace. We wish to live in love. We wish to live in happiness. Finally, we say, "Please, God, give me peace!" Or "Please, Buddha, give me happiness!" Son of a gun! This does not work. It's like planting tomato seeds and praying to God or Buddha to give you eggplants. So, if we wish to have eggplants, why not make the effort to plant the seeds so eggplants will grow? How can we do this? By listening to and reading Buddhist wisdom and the teaching of other spiritual leaders? This may help somewhat. But if this is not actualized into our lives, it remains an intellectual understanding and does not really come into the essence of our lives.

WHAT DO FLOWERS TELL US?

"Better than living a hundred years is one day in the life of a man who sees the highest truth." It is true. "If a man, causing pain to others wishes to obtain pleasure for himself, he, entangled in the bonds of selfishness, will never be free from hatred." It is; it is.

We read these beautiful words of wisdom from the Dhammapada. Through reading and listening we know the teachings of Buddha and the teachings of other great teachers as well. But living with *this*, actualizing *this* into our lives, is completely different from knowing about *this*. The trouble is we know so much; we have read books and heard so many talks. Wc have heard so many words of wisdom from tapes and speeches.

If *this* is not actualized into your life, *it* remains an intellectual understanding and does not really come into the essence of your life. You can say, "I know it. I have read such and such a book." That's fine.

The words of others can enrich your life. But unless you mix words and wisdom in your life, the words are only floating on the surface of the water. The words have to sink into the water which is your life. If you concentrate on one thing and actualize this practice into your life, you will see the joy of life and the meaning of all the teachings.

We cannot ignore the true meaning of our lives. We sometimes live like we are already dead, chasing after all kinds of material abundance. Gaining material things is important, as long as we need them. "Though one should conquer in battle thousands and thousands of men, whoso shall conquer himself is the greatest of warriors." It is true, isn't it? It's easy for me to get a gun and shoot you, thus conquering you. We can always buy a powerful weapon. But conquering one's self is the hardest thing to do.

Here are some beautiful magnolia flowers. Magnolias come in different shapes and colors. In New Haven, Connecticut, I walked down a street where there were magnolia trees on either side of the street. There were white, blue, purple, dark purple, like these. They were beautiful!

I can't resist saying my favorite poem again:

Roses are blooming on the rose bush.
There is nothing strange.
The flower blooms silently and falls quietly
    without sound,

Never again to return to its branch.
Her total existence is expressed in that one moment,
One place on the branch.
That is the voice of the flower,
The truth of the single flower on the branch.
Therein lies the joy of life, infinitely brilliant and
      everlasting.

You are living your life. There is nothing strange. "The flower blooms silently and falls quietly without sound, never again to return to its branch." The flower is silent. It is not saying, "Hey, hey, hey, you're ugly and I am beautiful. I have five petals, but you only have four! I am longer than you are, I am more powerful than you are! Look, one of your petals is shrinking and mine is not!" This one branch has a flower on it, and the flower does not know when these petals will fall. Maybe, as we leave this service, these petals will fall. Perhaps it will be tonight. The petals are not saying, "Hey, I might fall tonight."

This flower stem has been cut so it is not rooted in the ground. Even if this stem was rooted in the ground, it's a sure thing that this petal will fall to the ground. The flower will wilt and fall. Shakyamuni Buddha said, "You are living in a burning house." What does it mean? The house is your life. You are living in a burning life. The house may burn down within one hour, two hours. Do you realize it?

You will not live forever. Suppose you are fifty years old? I don't know how long you will live. Maybe until you are seventy-five? You are living in a burning house. Realize it! When you realize it, you know what to do. When you don't realize it, you don't know what to do. Some people say they want to die or they say, "I want to die when I am sixty." But whether you say you want to live or to die, you will surely die. You may want to die, but unless the time comes, you won't die. So don't worry about it.

"The flower blooms quietly and falls quietly without sound, though never again to return to its branch." This, too, is a beautiful part of this poem, don't you think? The flower does not return to the same branch. You don't go back to the same situation, the same conditions. Your life is the flower on the branch. "Her total existence is expressed in that one moment." Her total existence in that one moment is expressed on one place on the branch. Are you totally expressing your life on your branch? That's a good question!

Be the best of yourself, without comparison with others. It's easy to say, but hard to do. When we realize it, it is the only thing you can do. Each one of us has different conditions and situations, a different life. Have you ever been a patient in a hospital? Even with such limitations, you can be the best of yourself. At such times the nurses and doctors are working, using modern technology. Someone who is in touch with the essence of life is able to feel the interrelationship between such a situation and the voice of this flower. The voice of the flower is expressed in this place, at this moment. This single flower, on its branch, expresses the absolute truth. "Therein lies the joy of life, infinitely radiant and everlasting."

I frequently tell myself and my students:
Don't be so serious.
Don't lose your sense of humor.
Don't lose your sincerity.

THREE IMPORTANT MATTERS

I observe people today in America. Most are so serious. When people are so serious, they tend not to be patient enough, kind enough, thoughtful enough and not mindful enough to oneself or to others. A few weeks ago, I watched the news on TV. A driver did not start his car right away when the stop light turned to green. The man in the car behind honked his horn, then he got out of his car, argued with the driver of the first car and shot him to death. This is an extreme example, but it is a good example of how we are becoming too serious, short tempered and losing patience.

Often it is easy for so-called religious people to become so serious, fanatic even, and lose a broader vision of the essence of religion. A good question is: *What is the purpose for which we practice religious and spiritual teaching?* Meditation practice and listening to the teaching of Buddha is nothing but to know oneself, to open oneself, to open up one's self-centeredness and to expand into the vast openness or immeasurable light of compassion and wisdom. It is like a small river of self that streams into a vast ocean and becomes one taste of wisdom and compassion.

We ought not to lose our sincerity or heart in whatever we do and say. When we lose our sincerity, we take advantage of others and lose heart-felt relationships with people, other beings, plants even. If we lose our sincerity, then times when we are having dinner with friends, drinking together, and having sexual intercourse with a loved one will become robot-like actions. There will be no warm feelings. This sincerity or heart will be naturally built up when you practice feeling the stream of self flowing into the ocean of wisdom and compassion. Or you may call this ocean Buddha or love or God.

Finally, we should not lose a sense of humor in our daily life as well as in our religious or spiritual practice. A sense of humor helps keep a healthy spirit. A sense of humor guides our small ego to become dynamic and produces a creative way of life.

Here is a story from my life. It is not a serious interaction between myself and another. Rather it demonstrates sincere or heartfelt interactions between myself and another.

A man had parked his car in the temple's parking lot on a snowy evening. At about 11:00 in the night I heard the spinning of wheels as the man tried to get his car moving. I looked out the kitchen window and thought, "Poor guy, he's stuck in the snow." My first thought was that he should not have parked his car in our parking lot. Then I felt sorry for him as he struggled in the cold and snow to get his car from being stuck. I put a coat over my pajamas. I went out of the house with a shovel and helped him get his car out of the snow.

He gave me a big smile and said, "I know Chinese people are very kind."

I said, "Hey, I'm Japanese!"

He said, "Japanese people are even kinder."

I said, "Wait a moment, I'm Chinese."

Confused, he said, "You're funny!"

There was a pause and I said, "It does not matter if I am Japanese or Chinese. I am Mr. Kindness."

We laughed.

He said, "You are strange."

He said, "You are strange."

I said, "You are strange, too."

The man smiled, thanked me and left.

Helping this man get his car unstuck in the snow was just kindness; it was doing something. Who cares if the person extending kindness is Chinese or Japanese? Someone bothered to come out of his warm house to shovel snow so this man could get his car moving.

This man came to temple on Sunday. He called me on the phone from time to time and said, "Hey, Reverend, how are you doing?" After a couple of years he told me he was moving to Houston. He still sends me Christmas cards. Interesting experience, isn't it?

Don't be so serious.

Don't lose your sincerity.

Don't lose your sense of humor.

Six

How can I take care of
my passions and delusions?

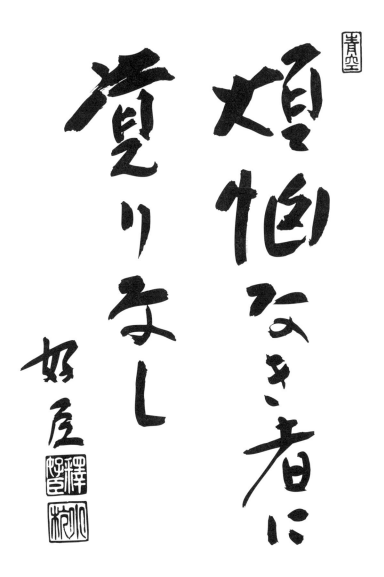

" The one who does not have Dukkha,
worldly passions,
does not have the opportunity
of enlightenment"

What we learn is always the kind of life
we are creating.   That's a key point.
I'm not saying which experiences; I'm
saying all experiences.   This is very
hard to understand through our
intellectual analysis.   When we realize
the light of wisdom and compassion, we
spontaneously and noticeably change.

DUKKHA AND MY PASSIONS AND DELUSIONS

Here are 108 small beads circling around my palms.   In Buddhist thinking they stand for 108 desires.   Thousands of years ago, people in India analyzed our emotions, our passions and illusions into 108 of them.   So don't get excited when you feel one or two of them.   There are 108!   When I wear these beads, putting palms together, I make an honest presentation of myself. I am living with passions, illusions, desires, anger and folly.

The 108 desires, which these beads represent, are divided into three categories or phases.   The first stage is endless wanting, the second stage is anger which occurs when the desires are not fulfilled, and the third stage is regret.   These are very normal phases for us human beings to go through as we live our daily lives.   Here is an example to show you how these phases operate.

Suppose you are attracted to a young woman and you take her on a date.   You buy her flowers and dinner.   At the end of the date she just says, "Thank you and good night," and goes rapidly into her home.   You've been raised well, so you accept this behavior at the end of the first few dates.   After many such dates you begin to think, "I spent such time and money and she still only says *Thank you and good night* at the end of the date.   I want more than this!"   You get angry.   Then you feel regret.   You may think, "I should never have taken this woman on all those dates." You may think, "I spent a lot of money on her; she is not worth it!"

I think as we live, we all have endless desires, desires for eating and drinking, sleeping, material things, sexual experiences and fame. Now you may not think of sleeping as something to be desired. Then go for one night without sleep. If you still don't understand, go a second night without sleep. Then you'll probably say to your wife or husband, "Honey, leave me alone! I want some sleep." There is also endless desire of eating; yes, eating is fun.

And we have desire for material abundance. Business people are very smart to take advantage of such desire in people, presenting fashions and more fashions. Do you know that people buy new expensive golf clubs each year because golf club companies produce new styles each year? Their advertisements say things like, "If you buy this, you can hit the ball straight." We want to be like that, so we buy new clubs. There is also endless desire for prestige. It is nice to be admired with titles, names and fame. There is also endless desire for sex. This is not good or bad, it just is endless. But when these things don't go as I wish, then the trouble begins.

To me these 108 passions and desires represent the energy and power of life. That does not mean that having passions and desires makes us bad or good, right or wrong; so it is, so these endless desires are. These two large beads symbolize wisdom and compassion. So I question myself *Practicing wisdom and compassion, what does that mean?* To me these 108 desires are the energy of life, the power of life. There is no question about it.

In Buddhist practice we often talk about casting away or decreasing such emotions and thoughts as greed, anger and delusion. But I want to talk about *Dukkha* and practicing *without working to cast away or destroy our passions and delusions. These passions and delusions are the power of living.*

The Buddhist term *Dukkha* is sometimes translated into English as *illusions.* But this definition does not explain *Dukkha* well. *Dukkha* is endless anger, endless desire, endless idle complaints. We usually practice in order to reduce or cast away things like greed, anger and folly. We practice to decrease what in Buddhist terminology is called Dukkha or illusions. One sutra says that without putting effort into cutting these out of your life, you can live in the state of mind of perfect harmony, the mind of enlightenment. This is puzzling, isn't it? You are making such an effort to decrease passions and delusions. You attend a workshop; you learn techniques to reduce or cut off what is in your mind in order to attain peace of mind. But now you hear that without getting rid of passions and delusions, you can live in a state of mind of perfect harmony, the mind of enlightenment. How could I be like that?

I have practiced the Buddha Dharma over 55 years and I have lived with endless desires, passions, greed, anger, follies and idle complaints. From the ordinary sense, this goes on and on, never concluding. So I question myself *What am I doing?* Even Zen masters get mad; other great people get mad. As long as they are living as human beings, they are living with such endless desires, anger and folly.

Because we think of putting effort into getting rid of Dukkha, someone may take advantage of you or me, especially from a religious viewpoint. It is easy to do.

You may think Sensei Ogui will not get mad; he is enlightened. Oh yes, I don't get mad the first time something doesn't go my way. Even the second time. But the third time is my limit. I tell my adopted daughter that I can repeat things three times, but if I have to repeat something four times, you should know I am getting mad. She remembers this and tells me, "I can play around until the fourth time, then you will get mad."

Feeling anger and passion is an endless reactive chain as we live. These exist to the last moment of our death. It does not matter if you are Buddhist or Christian or Hindu or atheist. This still happens to you.

So how can I live in a state of enlightenment? Here is one answer to this dilemma. Think about the properties of light. It shines everywhere on everyone! It even shines on people you don't like. Yes, clouds may come between you and sunlight, but eventually the sun will break through and shine on you. This light, which is always shining, has the power to change or transform a bitter apple to a sweet apple without changing the form of the apple. This kind of change is possible through awareness, understanding and realization. Awareness can change the direction of your life. With awareness the light of wisdom and compassion starts working. You could say that such energy, the energy of Dukkha, can be transformed into the energy of enlightenment.

It is like an apple. It is very sour at the beginning. The sun shines on the apple and changes the apple. The taste of the apple changes from bitter to sweet. The apple is transformed. So anger, desire and folly are the energy of life. If we can transform ourselves, desire, anger and folly become the power of awareness and enlightenment.

Then I question, how can I do this? It could be by awareness. Yes, I have to be aware. We may think that to be aware, we have to learn, study and practice. But true learning comes from life experiences. *Life is practice.*

We usually think the good, happy aspects of our lives are *mine*. This kind of understanding is hardly learning. With this approach, it takes enormous time. Maybe not learning anything even. But get rid of good and bad and right and wrong. Thus, whatever happens in your life, see it, face it, overcome it. Then always question, "What do I learn from this experience?"

What we learn is always the kind of life we are creating. That's a key point. I'm not saying which experiences; I'm saying *all* experiences. This is very hard to understand through our intellectual analysis. When we realize the light of wisdom and compassion, we spontaneously and noticeably change.

It is easy to talk about faith, but emphasizing faith can lead you away from spiritual awareness. You have to have a balance of understanding and faith. Having faith is a short cut, but this faith has to be unconditional. You have to throw yourself into it. No questions, no conditions. Then you live in it. That's the dangerous part, and yet very powerful part, because the light of wisdom and compassion has power. It is usually analyzed into three different ways. The first two we hear people talk about as self-power and other power. This "third power" is the power to take in. You are taken into the light. Even though you say *No, thank you, no, no, no. I don't need it*, you are already taken in. You are transformed and ripened like a sweet apple. In the light of the third power, there is no first and second, there is the power to break the darkness. You have to abandon yourself. That's quite a gamble.

Suppose you have made the effort to climb up too high, say climb up to the peak of a pole. Perhaps you have made the effort to practice with Zen Shin Sangha at the Cleveland Buddhist Temple. At the top of the pole one may hear a voice, Take one more step forward, one more step, one more. You think, "No, no." You don't know what will happen. This experience is very strong.

Last Sunday I talked with people with AIDS who came to the service. Many of them were very firm in their speech. When I go to visit such people, I go with the idea that I am a clergyman going to comfort them. Usually I am comforted *by* them. I feel great when I am with them because they don't worry about what may happen after life or before life and so on. They are perfectly in their life, right then. They don't even need a name. We need a name, a life of compassion, we need the powers of God and Buddha and so on. But they don't think they need any of these. They are left perfectly in the flow of their lives.

One time I was lying down in my living room, watching TV, and a swimming instructor was saying, "Hey, don't struggle, don't struggle. Relax, relax, then you'll float. The more you struggle, the more you sink." I thought *Wow! What is this?* You could try it next summer. You could swim in a pool and try it. When we struggle, the more we thrash around and move, we sink fast. When we watch professional swimmers, they are so relaxed. They float to the surface and just move. They are so relaxed. We so often struggle to cast away our energy of anger, follies and desire. But instead, just accept it, see it as *what I am*. This does not mean to intentionally do things that hurt other people.

From there you are taking the first step. Learn from the experience, the teaching, the practice. Build up the power of wisdom and compassion. This assists us to transform. It is possible to be transformed by awareness. Through awareness, it is possible to change your way of life, to change your character, to change your lifestyle or to change your way of thinking.

Yet we always go back again and again. Then you could smile, and when you smile, you come back again. This part is very difficult, very difficult. You're in a cycle. So maybe at the end of the beginning of old age, you may learn to throw yourself into the power of light, wisdom and compassion. Then you flow. This is the means to enlightenment without cutting off such Dukkha or illusions which are endless. You can live in the life of enlightenment, the life of harmony.

That's all I can explain at the present time. Maybe I could do better tomorrow, but for today it is the best I can do. Did you understand some of it? The one thing I encourage myself and I encourage you also -- do not conclude anything. Being a conclusion-seeker is a modern sickness. Be aware that we are living in the process of becoming. That's the reason why I said I may explain it better tomorrow. But I won't be here tomorrow.

I will do the best I can without comparison to others.

ARE YOU HAPPY?

A couple of evenings ago I went to a Japanese restaurant here in Cleveland. I was sitting at the sushi bar, talking to some Japanese businessmen.

As I was talking and eating, a distinguished Caucasian man approached me. He said to me, "I don't want to bother you, but I have observed you on several occasions here at this restaurant and I'd like to ask you a question."

I felt his sincerity, so I said, "Yes, please."

"I've watched you several times here, even though you come here alone, you are always happy. How can you always be so happy? What makes you happy?"

I said, "I'm sorry that I don't know what you mean by *happy.*" Then I felt I should be a little more kind, so I phrased my words differently, "I don't have the consciousness of being happy or unhappy. I used to have such a consciousness." As we drank and ate he talked and talked and talked. He had so many preconceived ideas on happiness! I could tell he didn't realize what I was saying when I said, "I don't know what you mean by happy."

Have you ever stopped to think *What is happiness, anyway? Do you clearly understand what would make you happy and what would make you unhappy?* I think most people do not have a clear idea of what would make them happy. Yet each person wants to be happy. We each create ideas in our minds of what would make us happy and unhappy. Sometimes I do this too.

People ask us *Are you happy?* and expect an answer. We may say *Yes* or *Not much.* If you are happy, how much? Do you have 9.5 happies? I have been asked from childhood *Are you happy?* I feel responsible to respond to this question. Behind this question is the expectation that I *should* be happy. This creates frustration, especially when things don't go as I wish. I get depressed. When things go as I wish, I think *This is a good day. My day!* I feel uncertain, yet I think I am happy.

We usually think *I'll find a pretty congenial girlfriend* or *I'll find a handsome, rich boyfriend. That will make me happy.* Or *I'll buy a beautiful house. That will make me happy.* Suppose you may have to compromise and buy a smaller house. Would a smaller, less luxurious house make you happy?

Suppose you buy a new car. Would that make you happy? Since you bought the car, you will have to be concerned about the car being stolen. Also you have to buy insurance for the car. You may be involved in an accident. Then you would have the expense of the accident because you bought and drove the car. In addition, you could get a speeding ticket while driving the car. This car, which you bought to make you happy, may make you unhappy. In fact, the possibilities of this car causing you unhappiness are limitless. So will a new car make you happy?

Does marriage bring only happiness and bliss? Ask anyone who has been married for five years or more. Does having a child bring complete happiness? Ask someone raising a teenage child. We all experience the weather. Do certain weather conditions make us happy? Take snow, for example. One man is happy when it snows because he loves to ski or because his business is snow plowing and he wants to make some money. Another man hates the snow because of the cold and the difficulty it causes him in driving. So does snow bring happiness or unhappiness?

You may still say, "I have to be happy." We think, "Yes!" Our culture is very affirmative. Our culture emphasizes that each of us *should* be happy. In thinking this way we dichotomize or use our minds to separate experiences in our lives. This is what we do when we categorize aspects of our lives as *happy* or *unhappy*. In contrast, I said to the man in the restaurant, "I don't know what is happiness or unhappiness."

Here is an interesting practice. Think about what would make you happy. Attach to it. Hang on to it in your mind. Examine it. See it. Then try to figure out what is happiness or unhappiness in the absolute sense. Then surely you will *hit the wall* in your mind. When you make yourself an empty teacup, then you don't have to know what is happiness or unhappiness. Make yourself free from notions of happiness and unhappiness. Then you become full of appreciations for the experiences in your life. So why not practice to see things totally.

Forget about happiness and unhappiness. The Heart Sutra says, "No, no, no." It is full of negations. The secret of Buddhist wisdom is to negate all. In fact, complete negation is complete affirmation. I can make myself free from the conceptual limitations of happiness and unhappiness. Then a true sense of my life arises. Sometimes I feel sad, miserable even. Sometimes I feel content, joyous even. But there are no frustrations concerning being happy or unhappy. Interestingly, the man who observed me in the Japanese restaurant perceived me as being *happy*.

Our persistence in dichotomizing not only makes us categorize experiences as happy and unhappy, it also creates tensions spiritually. You may think *God will take care of me*. In thinking this you make God and yourself separate. Actually I think God gets tired of this kind of thinking. There are a lot of people in the world for him to take care of! When you truly negate the concept of God, then you are living in the love of God.

I want to *live* my life totally. I know my life will never occur again in the same conditions as right now, so I will do the best I can without comparison to others.

I think I am a smart human being. I have been to school and I have studied a great deal. In spite of this, I am able to open myself, to learn, to become aware, to guide myself into realization, enlightenment even. God's love is manifested in my life, so I rejoice to be a human being. I am as I am. I try not to lose my sincerity. I am living in oneness with Amida Buddha or infinite life and light. Here is a lifetime koan: *What does it mean to live in infinite life and light?*

On this bookmark which someone gave me, it says:
May you walk with grace. And may the light of the universe shine upon your path.

WHAT ABOUT GRACE?

We each walk with grace and kindness, which supports us and helps us. It is so! The light of the universe *does* shine on each of us. When we think this over, we know that we have been living in grace since before we were born.

The trouble is most of the time we are not aware of this. In the Summer people say, "It is hot." In the Winter, even while staying in warm, cozy houses, people look out the window and say, "It is cold." In the fall people say, "The leaves fall on the ground in my yard and mess up my garden." In the Spring people say, "All these flowers and green grass give me hay fever!" It is extremely easy to complain. Since we spend so much time complaining, I think a good question is *When do we enjoy our lives?*

In contrast, I was talking with one of you before the service. She said, "I was lucky I came to Cleveland, which was far from my parents, and went through a divorce." This sounds like an unusual thing to say, doesn't it? Please do not misunderstand what I am saying; I am not recommending divorce. This person was saying this because these experiences led her to search for spiritual meaning.

You may think that spiritual growth will take you to heaven. If you think you are among a selected few who are going to heaven, you are extremely selfish. I think it is better to go to hell. In hell there will be plenty of your friends. You could possibly help some of them. I think when you go to hell, then it is an excellent place to practice *loving your neighbor.* In hell you are freed from obligations as a father, mother, brother and sister and so on. This frees you up even more to love your neighbor.

Here is a story to illustrate why I think going to hell is preferable to going to heaven. There was a man who went to heaven. This man liked to play golf. While playing golf in heaven, the first ball he hit went right onto the green. His second hit went right into the hole on the green. When his turn came each time, the same thing happened. His first stroke hit the ball onto the green. His second hit also went right into the hole. In fact, every ball he hit went right where he wanted it to. Since the golf course was in heaven, the people with whom he was playing also had all their balls go into the hole on the green on the first stroke of the club. The man said, "What kind of a golf course is this? This is boring. I want to go to a different golf course." His friend said, "Go to hell; hell has a different golf course."

When this man went to hell and played golf, all the balls did not go into a hole on the first hit. In hell, things would not go as he wished. Thus, in hell, this man would feel the joy of making an effort to improve his golf game.

What do you do when things don't go as you wish? How do you act at such times? We can learn from loneliness, anger, disappointment, sickness and arguing with others. Yes, sometimes I may think this experience is hard for me. Then I ask myself *What can I learn from this experience?* This is the attitude of someone seeking the meaning of life. Each experience in my life is a gift, a chance to learn and advance my spiritual life. I try not to ignore each experience, no matter how painful.

Last night many of us came to celebrate Obon here at the Cleveland Buddhist Temple, we had dancing on the lawn and great food to eat. It was beautiful -- young children, adults, older people, people of different races -- all were spending the evening together. Were you able to enjoy it? Or were you worried about problems in your life? Each of our lives is uniquely different. But opportunities for growth are given to each one of us. We each *do* walk in grace. The light of the universe *is* shining on the path of each one of us.

So do not look for grace, nor the light of the universe! We have been living in grace and in the light of the universe! When do we become aware of this?

I was born as the eighteenth generation Buddhist priest, so I was brought up in a temple. When I was a child, a guest priest came to the temple and spoke three times a day: in the morning, afternoon and in the evening for a week. He told the same stories over and over concerning Na man da bu, infinite compassion and wisdom or infinite light and life. As the week wore on, fewer and fewer people came to hear him. At the end of the week he told the few people who were there, "Now you can make it your own."

NEMBUTSU

I'm going to tell you a story which I have told before. I will continue to tell stories over and over, you listen until you can make them your own.

I do not make up stories . . . too much. One chapter in the Buddhist Sutras is called Hoben-Bon, Chapter of Good Lie. The stories in this chapter are not really lying, but rather they are *means to get in touch with the essence or bridges to the essence.* I'll explain further.

You have a picture of your father. The picture is a piece of paper, it's not your father. Your father is not exactly as you see him in the picture rather he is changing every moment. He is changing physically, spiritually and psychologically.   Even though the picture is not an exact likeness of your father as he is now, you can get in touch with the feelings you have toward your father through the picture. So the picture is a means through which you can get in touch with the feeling of your father.

Another example is this statue of Shakyamuni Buddha on the altar of this temple. It is a figure or image of a human being which has nothing to do with the man Shakyamuni Buddha. This gold statue is a symbol of enlightenment, but enlightenment has no form or color. The materials in this statue temporarily have this form. This form is a means to get in touch with the essence of enlightenment or, in other words, infinite wisdom and compassion.

So my stories, both the ones from my life and the ones I make up, are means or bridges to help you get in touch with the Buddha Dharma, but you need to make them your own flesh and blood.

Here is a true story from my life. I was minister of a large temple in San Francisco. I had a call in the daytime from a man who is a second generation Japanese American. This man said, "Sensei, my father is dying. He asked me to call you to come."

I drove through the traffic in San Francisco. The atmosphere in a hospital, especially in a room where people are dying, is entirely different. You can't walk into a room in which someone is dying and say, "Hi! How are you doing?" Actually, whether people are aware of it or not, they are changed by such an atmosphere. Ministers and counselors working with dying people and their families are quite exhausted after such encounters due to these drastic changes in energy.

When I walked into the hospital room of the dying man, I heard family members crying. The man dying was an Issei pioneer, a first generation Japanese American. His son said, "Papa, priest is here."

With his whole strength the dying man extended his hand to shake my hand. I shook his extended hand. I noticed he was saying something, so I got close to him. He said, "Thank you very much for all kinds of things."

I kept quiet. I couldn't find any adequate words to describe my feelings. I shook his hand tightly.

The son with tears in his eyes said, "Papa, I shall see you again in the Pure Land. I learned this in Sunday school."

I knew that this son is a doctor in biochemistry and teaching at Stanford University. I thought to myself, "I've never seen this guy at the temple, but he must have been a Sunday school kid when he was younger."

I was quiet.

The dying man began talking with all his strength, "Say, my son, do I have to go to some other place to meet you again? I have already met you and I'm meeting with you in Nembutsu. Na man da bu. Na man da bu."

There is actually no way to describe what I experienced. At that moment, there was a golden quietness. I was quiet, with no intention to be quiet. I was astonished. I shook his hand again.

After the moment, my computer brain began to analyze so I could describe the feeling I experienced. I felt as if I was facing a magnificent scene like the Canadian Rockies. I felt as if I was swallowed or taken into these gigantic snow peaked Canadian Rockies. I scared myself even.

As I drove from the hospital I felt so enriched. The dying Issei's words echoed in my mind. *Do I have to go to another place to meet you again? I have already met you and am meeting with you in the realization of oneness of Nembutsu. Na man da bu. Na man da bu.* How fortunate I am, working as a so-called Buddhist minister. I have such great opportunities to meet and learn from people.

I have been well-trained at the Yale Divinity School to give final prayers. I had thought I had gone to the hospital to comfort this dying man. Clergy are supposed to say words of wisdom which comfort people, you know. I had not spoken even one word to him. *He gave wisdom to me. He manifested the truth to me!*

Most patients are extremely insecure and uncertain when dying. In contrast, this man simply, maturely, firmly shared wisdom and compassion with me, the clergyman. He did this without any intention to do so. What wisdom he lived! His spiritual life was so enriched. There was no need for final prayers for this Issei pioneer. He is the one who lived in the eternal moment in a realization of oneness with self and non-self.

That evening I received a call from his son. He said, "My father passed away."

After the memorial service, the son came to me and said, "I still don't understand the meaning of what my father said. What did he mean when he said he has already met with me in the realization and oneness of Nembutsu? Na man da bu."

I said to this son, "Since you are a professor and you give homework to your students, I leave this question to you as your lifetime homework."

As I thought about the way I answered this son's question, I smiled to myself. And now, my friends, I give you the same lifetime homework. Make it your flesh and blood.

Do I have to go to another place to meet you again? I have already met you and am meeting with you in the realization of oneness of Nembutsu. Na man da bu. Na man da bu.

What is this?

Note: *Na man da bu*, in this case is the sound of oneness with myself and Amida Buddha.   Amida Buddha means infinite life and light. The infinite life manifests in our life as infinite compassion and the infinite light manifests as infinite wisdom.

We all want peace and harmony. Yes, there are people in this world who are destroying the peace and harmony. Also, there are people who are creating peace and harmony in this planet. You came here to meditate and in other ways, we are building up peace and harmony. As long as we can maintain the balance of destroying and creating peace and harmony, we may keep up a reasonable life on this planet. However, because of our desires and self-concerns, at times we cannot help but do actions which disrupt the peace and harmony.

ARE YOU GRATEFUL THAT YOU HAVE NOT KILLED EVEN ONE PERSON?

I want to extend the notion of peace and harmony in this world by telling you about a teaching of Shinran. Shinran brought Buddhist teachings from the monasteries in the mountains of Japan to people in the less mountainous areas. He brought the teachings to ordinary people who had families, struggling to make a living, engaging in day-to-day conflicts with each other. His message is particularly useful as we live our stress-filled lives in America today.

One day Shinran called one of his disciples to him and asked, "Have you ever killed a person?"

The disciple said, "No, I've never killed any person."

Shinran asked, "Do you respect me as your teacher? Will you do what I ask of you?"

The disciple said, "Of course, I do."

Shinran replied, "Then go out and kill a hundred people."

The disciple was frightened by this. He doubted what he had heard. He was quiet. Then the disciple humbly said, "Even though you ask me to kill a hundred people, I cannot kill even one person."

Shinran smiled and said, "Why can't you kill even one person?"

The disciple was quiet. He couldn't find an answer. He wondered, "Why can't I kill even one person?"

Shinran said, "Is it because of your good will or your good heart or because you are a good person?"

The disciple still could not answer.

After a short silence Shinran said, "It is not because you have a good mind or even a good heart or because you are a good person. You are fortunate because present conditions and situations do not allow you to kill even one person. Aren't you grateful that your present conditions and situation are such that you do not have to kill even one person? If the conditions and situations changed, you don't know what you would do."

This is an interesting message, isn't it? You probably think, "I'm not that kind of person who would kill even one person. I am a good Christian or I am a good Buddhist. You know not to kill is a Buddhist Precept as well as a Christian Commandment. But Shinran is saying you don't do heinous actions like killing a person, *not* because of such a mind or will, but because you are very fortunate that conditions and situations are not such that you would kill even one person.

We don't know what we might do in unexpected conditions and situations. Take the example of a bomber pilot during World War II. He simply pushed a button and killed millions of people with a bomb. He may have said, "I just pushed a button. I didn't do anything. I was just following orders." This same man may have gone home and walked in on his wife as she was being raped. What would this man do in this situation? Whatever his actions, would he say as he did before, "I didn't do anything"? Would he justify his actions?

What Shinran wanted his disciple to reflect on concerned being thankful he had not been in such conditions and situations as these. Shinran's disciple was not in such an extreme situation like being a bomber pilot or seeing his wife being raped.

Let's look at a less extreme example. Once I saw an expensively dressed lady driving a Jaguar in a fashionable residential area. She didn't stop at a red light and ran through it. Her car was almost hit by another car. Her face got red with anger at the person driving the other car. I could tell she was not grateful even though she had barely missed being hit. I wondered how this physically beautiful woman talked with her husband about the near collision when she got home.

Most of us have experienced driving a car and almost being hit by another car. I smile at myself, observing my reaction after such occurrences. Observing how we react in such situations is an interesting practice.

Sometimes I would like to run away from myself or disappear. But I can't. I have to live with myself. I cannot get tired of myself. So I have a consciousness to live with myself and to learn from any experience. And I keep going and I encourage myself. I also have a consciousness to not conclude anything. I think conclusion-seeking is a modern sickness. Instead of becoming a conclusion seeker, we better realize that we are living in the process of becoming, changing and thus keep going. We have to learn to move on.

We don't know what will happen the next moment even. But we are here at this place at this moment. Whatever situations we are in, sadness or happiness, why not learn from it and nourish our self spiritually? Life is what I'm thinking and what I'm doing right now.

Does this make sense? I hope you are confused. I think a good confusion is like thinking about Shinran's thinking of being grateful when conditions are such that we do not do hateful actions. Good confusions make good questions. So often we become so fixed in our thinking. Then we become hard-headed. Small arguments become enlarged in our minds. You may say something hateful and get into a fight. You may even shoot and kill someone. So, as you live your life, think about such questions as *Are you grateful that you have not killed even one person?*

Even though there are people with rigid thinking, there are also concerned people who care. The Parliament of World Religions was hosted by concerned people living in the Chicago area. There are always concerned people. It is not a matter of Christian, Buddhist or Jewish, but rather concerned people who see the importance of sharing time with others of different traditions.

As I met with other religious leaders, I smiled at myself a lot, and I saw my ego reacting a lot. I learned from my experiences during the World Parliament of Religions. Though we wore different clothes related to our differing religious beliefs, we met together for three hours a day for three days. We ate the same food. We talked to each other and shared ideas. We are all human beings; each one of us has one life to live. It is indeed true that conditions allowed me to attend this conference.

I feel fortunate that I was able to participate in the Parliament of World Religions in Chicago.

Part of compassion or love is appreciating and enjoying the time we spend with others. True compassion, true love, involves letting others be as they are.

POSSESSING A FLOWER?

Here is a very beautiful flower. We love this flower, don't we? Living in Cleveland, springtime brings a joyous feeling. After we have experienced cold, snow and rain, bright sun-shiny days are glorious to us. People who live in Arizona, where the weather is temperate all year round do not experience the exuberance of springtime that we do. Flowers such as this one are so much a part of spring in Cleveland.

We are so possessive and selfish. We feel we cannot be secure unless we possess something we love. You love this flower; you love springtime. So try to possess them! This flower won't last forever, just as your life and the lives of those you love won't last forever. You cannot do too much. What kind of power do you have to make this flower bloom?

You may think, "I want to control everything, then I'll feel secure. I want to control my girlfriend, my children and my friends. I even want to control when this flower will bloom." You may think, "Flower, wait to bloom because my friend is coming from New York next weekend. Then you may bloom." You laugh. You know that you cannot control when and how long this tulip will bloom.

This tulip is blooming brightly for this Sunday service. For the Tuesday night Zazen Meditation Class it will be drooping somewhat and for the Wednesday evening class it will droop even more. So this flower is blooming, yet changing. Things are changing and becoming from moment to moment. Why can't we realize this?

This tulip is not blooming only for you alone. Spring has come to all people in the Cleveland area without discrimination. Yes, I can see, enjoy and appreciate this flower. I can realize that the beauty of spring surrounds me, that *I am taken into the beauty of this flower; I am taken into the radiance of springtime.* Yes, I can love this flower, but I cannot possess and control its life.

In so-called Buddhist terminology the term *compassion* is used rather than the term *love*. Part of compassion or love is appreciating and enjoying the time we spend with others. True compassion, true love, involves letting others be as they are. It involves understanding others, acting thoughtfully and respecting the choices that others made in their lives. Yes, as we love and appreciate this flower, we can love others and feel compassion toward them, but we need to realize that we cannot possess them.

Good morning. Nice to see all of you here this morning. We are all alive so that we are able to see each other like this. We don't usually think about how we are still alive. We take this for granted. But it seems to me, since we are put into such conditions and situations, then being alive and meeting with each other is meaningful.

Once I walked into a crematory and watched a body being burned. I did this to get a strong impact that I, too, will one day die. Because of this consciousness, I am able to see the significance of life itself, so I feel it is great to be here and meet with you. We each are living. We each are not dead yet. When I am faced with something I do not expect, something difficult, a hardship, this kind of consciousness is useful.

LET'S GO BACK TO THE BASICS!

Let's go back to the basics! What does this mean in terms of Buddha Dharma? Particularly Buddha Dharma here in America where we live together with such diversity of cultural backgrounds. What does going back to basics mean to us?

It means going back to the basic principles behind *all* religions. This will lead us to a harmonious way to understand each other. Individuals who profess each religion in this world are seeking peace and security for themselves and the ability to love and feel compassion for others. The purpose of every religion is to provide guidance for us to take care of our lives and to live in harmony with others.

Let's go back to a basic understanding of each one's life taught by Shakyamuni Buddha twenty-five hundred years ago. What he taught continues to make sense today in twentieth century America. Shakyamuni Buddha talked about the law of nature or Universal Truth. When Shakyamuni Buddha was enlightened, he deeply realized that *things are changing, becoming and moving on.* This is called the Law of Impermanence. Things change according to causes and conditions created by each of us. This Universal Truth applies to each one's life, so simply realize that things are changing, becoming and moving on. We have what is called *ignorance* at times when we do not see, when we do not understand and when we do not realize this truth. Ignorance causes suffering. Thus, we create our own suffering. Acceptance will not come through at times when we don't see or don't want to see, when we don't understand or don't want to understand, when we don't realize or don't want to realize. To alleviate our suffering we need to accept things as they truly are. When we fully realize things as they truly are, acceptance effortlessly becomes one's life.

So a basic question is, "How do I live with this law of impermanence?" We are each unique, so different from each other, so we each have different ways of living with the Law of Impermanence. We each have developed different habits. Even identical twins growing up in the same family are not exactly alike. Each of you reacts in a different manner as you hear this Dharma talk. Someone is fascinated. Someone gains insight. Someone else thinks, "What the heck is he saying?" Someone does not learn anything. Someone may get mad even.

As people stay at the temple, some people grow spiritually. Others groan, complain and criticize. Others enjoy temple functions, participate in them and use their talents. Some help others. I am not saying that these people are good or bad. Rather I can see that each one is living his or her life. Though we are so different, we each wish to live our own lives to the best of our abilities. We each desire security and peace in our lives.

We each are attached to those we love. We cannot get away from our attachments. Our fate includes attachments to certain people. Many of us have pledged our love for each other in front of the altar. But love itself is changing and becoming. Sometimes love changes to anger and hate even. Many people fall in love and later end up fighting each other in divorce courts. We say such things as, "How could he fall in love with such a guy?" or "How could she be unfaithful to him?" But love is moving on. You don't have to believe this. Look within your life and around at others' lives and you can see that this is true.

Things are changing, becoming and moving on. So many people who were here fifteen years ago are now dead. There is a coolness to this Law of Impermanence. Universal Truth is manifested into our lives.

I'm sure you have experienced being separated from a brother or sister, an uncle or an aunt, a daughter or a son, or a dear friend, that is, someone you were attached to who died before you. You miss them. You think about your relationship with such a person and the times you shared together. Sometimes you laughed together. Sometimes you exchanged anger. You think, "He left me!" or "She left me!"

Things are changing, becoming and moving on. We think, "Hey! He is changing, but not me." Or we think, "You look young!" Whether people look young or old, each one is

changing, becoming and moving on. A man who is becoming
bald may think when he looks in the mirror, "Oh, no. That is not
what I'm used to seeing."

Likewise one of you may come to the Cleveland Buddhist
Temple or some other temple and think, "Oh, no! That is not
what I'm used to seeing. It is Zen Buddhism! I like Shin
Buddhism." Someone else may come and say, "Oh, no! That is
Shin Buddhism. I like Zen Buddhism." But when people from
Japan who live with traditional Zen practices or traditional Shin
practices come to the Cleveland Buddhist Temple, they do not
think the forms and practices we have here at the Cleveland
Buddhist Temple are either Zen or Shin. These forms and
practices are not totally Zen, they are not totally Shin. *These are
simply the forms here at the Cleveland Buddhist Temple.* These
forms and practices came out of my living, practicing and
teaching with Americans -- Indian Americans, Japanese
Americans, German Americans, Jewish Americans -- whatever!
Here at the Cleveland Buddhist Temple, Buddhist culture is being
blended with American culture. This is true for all Buddhist
groups in America. If you are courageous enough to see it and
understand it, you can realize this. Then you will experience the
form so naturally. Yet this form is not definite at all. This form
is changing, becoming and moving on.

Non-Japanese Americans have joined the Japanese
Americans who built and started this temple. Both the Japanese
Americans and the non-Japanese Americans appreciate, are
devoted to and are gaining an understanding of Buddha Dharma.
Here at the Cleveland Buddhist Temple we practice Buddha
Dharma. We each work toward respecting our own life and the
lives of others.

So as we live our lives, there are changes in our love relationships, in matters of physical health and life and death, and in our spiritual practices -- and in all aspects of our lives! We don't want to go along with the changes we don't like. But we can't help it. *Things will change whether we want them to or not.*

Some people have such a power to nourish their own lives and the lives of others. These people realize that things are changing, becoming and moving on. This realization leads to a life of wisdom and compassion. These people respect their own life and the lives of others.

Let's realize the law of impermanence and live in it. Let's realize things are changing and move on. This basic idea of Buddha Dharma is quite simple, but at times difficult to live.

Seven
What can I do with my
limited time and energy?

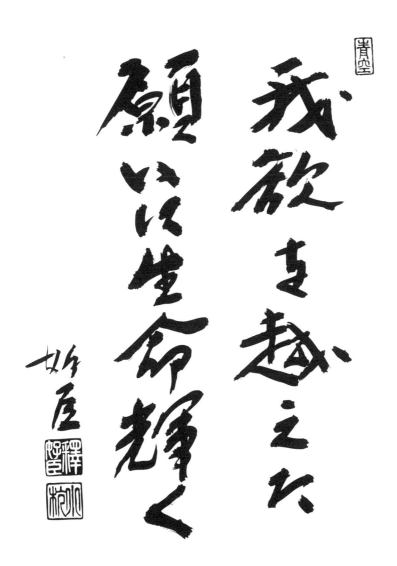

" Beyond one's selfish desire,
light shines on one's vow "

Buddha said, "Do not cry. I have always said that one must depart from loved ones. All living things must die. My death is only natural. That is why you must not continue to grieve. After I die, you must not depend on anything. The only thing you can depend on is yourself. Walk with your own legs, but you must walk one step at a time. One day there will come a time when you will be enlightened." That's quite a message, isn't it?

WHAT TO DO?

When the man Shakyamuni Buddha reached his 80th year, his health began to fail. He said to his followers, "Those with life must die. That is truly nature's way. Death is coming to me soon. But you must not continue to be sad."

The Buddha washed himself in the river and disciples made a place for him beside the river to lie down. The death of the Buddha approached. Ananda, a senior leader, approached the Buddha and said, "If anything should happen to you, what should we depend upon?" and Ananda started crying.

Buddha said, "Do not cry. I have always said that one must depart from loved ones. All living things must die. My death is only natural. That is why you must not continue to grieve. After I die, you must not depend on anything. The only thing you can depend on is yourself. Walk with your own legs, but you must walk one step at a time. One day there will come a time when you will be enlightened." That's quite a message, isn't it?

Then when death approached, many people came around. Buddha said, "Is there anything you want to ask me while you have the chance?"

The people became very quiet, weeping.

The Buddha continued, "All right, I see. It is so quiet. What is that sound?"

A disciple said, "It is the sound of water flowing."

Buddha said, "I see the river flows continuously, but the water flowing now is not the same water that flowed yesterday. The flow of the universe is the same. All things must change. You must all continue to put effort into realizing this so that you do not get left behind in this changing world."

Shakyamuni Buddha shared wisdom from his enlightenment for forty-five years. But this was Buddha's final message. When a disciple asked Shakyamuni Buddha, "What is the most valuable thing in this world? What good deeds will bring us peace and joy? What is the most beautiful taste of tastes in this world? How do you live to attain the highest life?", the Buddha answered, "In this world to awaken to the Dharma or Universal Truth is the most valuable thing in this world. The action of virtuous quality will bring us to peace and joy. The most beautiful taste of tastes is the truth. The highest life is to live by wisdom and compassion."

So this is part of the message to mankind left by the man Shakyamuni Buddha. But how do we follow the message he left?

Here is *one* way I will share with you. This afternoon I had time to lie on the couch and do nothing but watch TV. It has been a long time since I have done this. I was going out to play golf, but it was raining.

I watched the news. It's amazing. So many things are happening in this world -- killings, shootings. What a world we are living in! Where is love? Where is compassion and wisdom?

Look what grown-up, mature people are doing. Mature people abuse kids. A husband gets into drugs and beats up his wife.

I turned off the TV. I heard the dog barking. The cat stretched and walked into the kitchen where his cat dish is. I heard my neighbors talking and a fire engine or ambulance siren. I walked outside. I saw the blooming flowers moving in a gentle breeze.

Things are so as they are. Yet living as a human being, what can I do? I thought, "I could be like the almighty power of a savior. No, I can't." Then I questioned myself, "Can I enlighten myself? Can I save myself? No. Then how could I save others?" This is very presumptuous, isn't it?

Finally, I thought, "In such a limited time of life, in the space I am living, I will do what I can do." First, I fed the dog and took him outside so he could walk around. The dog was so happy! At least I could do something, even if it was small. Next I said, "Hi!" to my neighbor and shook his hand.

A well known saying in Japan is, "The one who brightens the corner is a national treasure."

Why not? Brighten one corner.

We can do all kinds of things at this moment of our lives.   At least at this moment we can put our palms together. Opportunities to become aware are equally given to each of us. We each have all kinds of experiences -- experiences which bring happiness, sadness, anxiety, anger, joy. Such experiences are equally given to everyone. The particular circumstances are different, but opportunities for awareness are equally given to each of us. Beautiful, isn't it?

EQUAL OPPORTUNITIES

Early this morning, Sandra came to talk to me. Sandra is the beautiful, African American girl sitting on the far side of the temple from where I am standing. She told me her grandma was in the hospital in intensive care. No one knows for sure if Sandra's grandmother will recover from her sickness and this is upsetting to Sandra.

She had said to me, "I don't know what to do." In reality there is nothing she can do to make her grandmother healthy. In such circumstances we worry and cry a lot. We become insecure and uncertain. We don't know what will happen.

People cry when a beloved child is ill or dead. This is a beautiful expression of human love. Yet, reality is often cruel. One person cannot give his or her life so a loved one can live. When our loved ones are ill, we often cry out. Friends try to calm us by sharing simple everyday actions like drinking a cup of coffee together. Our anguish affects others and they share in our worry. This is beautiful for others to have the same feeling to some degree. However, the bottom line is there is little we can do. Even doctors with modern technology at their fingertips have limitations of what they can do.

Even though there is nothing Sandra can do to make her grandmother healthy, she came to the temple early this morning to prepare the temple for this service. She put the chairs in order, prepared the altar, lit the candles and the incense. I told her I am proud of this. We each find ourselves in situations like this in which we *know* we can't do anything to change circumstances. But, like Sandra, we can know what we *can* do which will benefit ourselves and others. When we face a situation in which we don't know what to do, first don't do anything. Calm yourself down. Then, as Sandra must have done, say to yourself, "What can I do? Well, at least I can do this."

In Sandra's case, she came to the temple, set things in order and began welcoming people attending this service. I told her, "This is beautiful dedication, beautiful actions with sincerity." These actions are pure prayer, unconditional prayer, pure devotion. Such prayer and devotion has the power to transmit to others which will naturally benefit Sandra's grandmother. I will not argue how much. Putting energy into assisting others with sincerity is honorable. It makes a difference within us and for others for whom we care. Interesting awareness, isn't it?

We can do all kinds of things at this moment in our lives. At least at this moment we can put our palms together. Opportunities to become aware are equally given to each of us. We each have all kinds of experiences -- experiences which bring happiness, sadness, anxiety, anger, joy. Such experiences are equally given to everyone. The particular circumstances are different, but opportunities for awareness are equally given to each of us. Beautiful, isn't it?

We are often like a child when her mother asks, "What did you learn today at school?" This child says, "Mrs. Johnson is beautiful. I believe she was raised in a good family." The next day the mother asks the child again, "What did you learn today at school?" The child says, "Mrs. Johnson is smart. I believe she is the smartest teacher in the school." But what the mother wants to know is, *"What did my child learn?"*

DO NOT MISS THE POINT

People in the East, especially people in the Buddhist tradition, believe all beings are born with Buddha Nature. I was born with Buddha Nature, that is a nature to be one with wisdom, compassion and love. All beings have the ability to become a Buddha. This fan has Buddha Nature. Ridiculous, isn't it? It is just paper. Once a clock maker who is a friend of mine said, "Each clock has a life." My friend could see the life of the clocks. I couldn't see it. This was my level of spirituality concerning clocks. However, I know that all beings have the nature for enlightenment. You may wonder *How can I understand this?* A more important question is *How can I develop a feeling that all beings have Buddha Nature?*

I look at this picture of a dog one of you put up here. This dog has such great eyes. Eyes can talk a lot, you know. People who really live and share their lives with an animal like a dog don't need words to communicate with their dogs.

So dogs continue to love us even when we treat them roughly and we can communicate with our pets without using words.

These notions lead us to feelings of love and respect toward animals. This is important. On the other hand, it doesn't matter much if we believe that animals have Buddha Nature or not.

In the West we are taught religiously that God created us human beings in the image of God and that other beings are not created in the image of God. From this idea sometimes we think that we are superior to other beings. In a sense we believe we can control animals, that we can use them for our wishes, needs and wants. I am not saying that this belief is good or bad or right or wrong. Christian teachings and Buddhist teachings are not good or bad. We need to understand religious teachings, realize what they mean for our lives and then acceptance will come through. Sometimes people come up to me and say, "I am a Catholic," or "I am a Buddhist." Then I am at a loss for words. Or someone may say to me, "Are you a Buddhist?" Most of the time I cannot answer this. Sometimes I ask back, "What does a Catholic or a Buddhist look like?"

We are trained to attach to a name or a title, so we miss the essence of the teachings. Buddha is a savior; Jesus is the only savior. *But what do we learn from them?* We are often like a child when her mother asks, "What did you learn today at school?" This child says, "Mrs. Johnson is beautiful. I believe she was raised in a good family." The next day the mother asks the child again, "What did you learn today at school?" The child says "Mrs. Johnson is smart. I believe she is the smartest teacher in the school." But what the mother wants to know is *What did my child learn?* For example, did my child learn how to do a math problem or about the life of Martin Luther King or what? So the point is *what did you learn from Jesus, Mohammed or Buddha?* This is a key point.

Instead of looking at the essence of teachings, we, as human beings, have all kinds of beliefs, theories and concepts and we often base our actions on these theories. A lady called me up and told me that when her dog died she felt extremely sad, so she called her church for a service. The clergy said, "Dogs do not have a soul so there is no need for a service."

When we are freed from such concepts and beliefs, we can clearly see the life of animals, fish and birds. A cow in a slaughter house does not say, "I want to be eaten by people in Ohio." When I have gone into a medical research laboratory, I have a sense of sadness. No beings, including human beings, have a right to take other beings' lives.

Suppose a hungry superior being came to earth from another planet. This superior being sees some Asians and thinks, "Yummy! All the soy sauce they eat will make them very tasty for me to eat." Then this superior being sees some teenage Americans and thinks, "They will be good to eat also because they eat so many hamburgers and french fries." How does this scenario make us feel?

We need to realize the importance of other beings' lives. But we cannot help but take the lives of animals, fish and birds for food. Animals in the laboratory are killed to further medical research. It is not a matter of good and bad, but it is sad that we have to take others' lives for survival reasons, isn't it?

Once a medical research doctor talked to me about his feelings of guilt concerning killing animals while doing laboratory research. I said, "Think about sneaky guys like me. I do not work in a laboratory in which animals are killed. Yet I take medicine and I know that hundreds of animals have been killed in creating just this one medicine." People say, "I'm a vegetarian." But when we breathe, we take in the lives of hundreds of invisible beings without realizing it. When we take one step, we crush billions of microscopic living things. We need to understand and realize that *all* beings take others' lives for their own survival.

In fact, one way human beings are different from animals is that we can realize this fact and extend our love and respect for others' lives. We can feel sadness and gratitude for their sacrifice for our well being. Then we can work practically to minimize the taking of others' lives and feel responsibility for one's own life.

It is indeed true that one's life is not only one's life, but a life of others' sacrifices. How can I share my life with others? This is key point or a crucial awareness, isn't it? Do not miss the point; tell what you learned today.

Some people become too serious about their religious or spiritual practices and beliefs. Such people may think, "I know the answers. I have to save others." I say such people are "half enlightened." That's a funny expression, isn't it? Someone who is a little more enlightened may enjoy being by oneself and tend to get tired of talking to other people. A fully enlightened person works for oneself and others and feels joy in her work. Even so, we each live as emotional beings and so helping others is honestly tiring work. I have great respect for people who keep working, helping others. Maybe they are either quite devoted people or great stupid people, or both.

A HEART OF COMPASSION

Mother Teresa and Princess Diana both died. They touched our hearts. Their deaths moved us emotionally. I was thinking, "What does this mean to me that Mother Teresa and Princess Diana "moved us"? What came to my mind was that Mother Teresa and Princess Diana each lived a life based on *a heart of compassion*, yet lived so naturally.

Mother Teresa reminded me of an experienced Zen master. When people admired her, she didn't care. Of course, she appreciated it, but she always said, "Well, I'm not doing anything special. That's all that I can do." She lived with the poorest of poor. When she died, her funeral was like that of a king. She is a wonderful role model.

Princess Diana was charming. She fell in love, was divorced, felt much disappointment. She again fell in love. Because of these experiences, I felt close to her. I felt like I could say, "Hi, How are you?" to Princess Diana.

Both Princess Diana and Mother Teresa were gifted by their positions. Both of them acted in their positions in ways which showed a heart of compassion. They each knew to work for oneself and at the same time to work for others without any expectation. This is the true practice of Dana or sharing and giving. I cannot be like Mother Teresa nor like Princess Diana. Nor can you. We are not in the same positions and situations.

Yet we can have a heart of compassion. For example, this morning I stopped by a restaurant I frequent. The waitress said, "Hey, China Man, good to see you." She knows I am not Chinese and that I am a Buddhist minister; that is just what she calls me in a friendly way. She continued, "Hey, China man, I have a baby." And she showed me some pictures of her new baby.

This lady makes people who come to this restaurant feel joyous, particularly elderly people. She does not have a consciousness that she makes others feel bright. That's just what she does. I could not help myself, I gave her a twenty dollar bill and told her to buy something for her baby.

We can always ask ourselves *What can I do to make this life meaningful? What can I do to create a heart of compassion in myself?* By asking such questions of ourselves, we can work with ourselves to have a heart of compassion. Most of the time we waste energy a lot. If I don't feel like doing something with a compassionate heart, I open myself through letting go of worries and mind creations. Then the heart of compassion naturally arises.

Some people become too serious about their religious or spiritual practices and beliefs. Such people may think, "I know the answers. I have to save others." I say such people are "half enlightened." That's a funny expression, isn't it? Someone who is a little more enlightened may enjoy being by oneself and tend to get tired of talking to other people. A fully enlightened person works for oneself and others and feels joy in her work. Even so, we each live as emotional beings and so helping others is honestly tiring work. I have great respect for people who keep working, helping others. Maybe they are either quite devoted people or great stupid people, or both.

At least we could start by saying, "Hi!" to our friend. Let's be great stupid people.

There was once a traveler going through the forest. This traveler was shot with a poisoned arrow. One of his friends, who was with him, said, "I want to know who the man was who shot this arrow that hit my friend. I want to know if he was a Brahmin or from the Sudra caste. I want to know if he had a dark or light complexion. I want to know why he shot the arrow, what kind of bow he used and what kind of poison he used."

The man who was hit with the arrow had little time until the moment of this death. He said, "I only have a little time left to experience, to enjoy and to appreciate life. I have only a little time to seek the meaning of life." This dying man was guiding himself into spiritual awareness.

I WAS WATERING THE LAWN
BECAUSE IT WAS DYING

I was asked by a Catholic Priest, who heads the Interfaith Commission of Greater Cleveland, to write a short piece about the religious aspect of love. This short piece will introduce an interfaith conference on this topic. I asked him, "Why do you ask me to write about the religious aspect of love? I am very poor at writing English." He responded that the people in the Interfaith Commission had agreed to ask a Buddhist to write the introduction to the conference because Buddhism is a very universal religion. That made me very happy. My ego was very pleased to hear that!

In preparing to write this short piece, I looked over a pamphlet from the World Conference of Religions on Peace, a movement in which Reverend Tsuji in Washington, D.C. is deeply involved. I read some very beautiful messages from all the religions of the world, and the bottom line is that *all* religions stand for peace and love and understanding. So when you talk about religions, ask each other, "What is the bottom line? What is the point?"

Someone may say, "Yes, I believe in Jesus." That's fine, but what is the point? Someone else may say, "Mohammed is the final prophet." That's fine, but what is the point? Share it with me! Someone else may say, "I follow the Buddha." Yeah, that's fine, you have the freedom to follow anything, but what is the point? What is the bottom line? What is the Buddha teaching us?

People are getting tired and disgusted with religion. One reason this is happening is because religion becomes very exclusive. People talk about loving thy neighbor but practice only loving their friends; they bitterly criticize others with beliefs differing from theirs. But if people would look at themselves and consider *What can I do with my life?* then followers of each religion could live up to the principles of their religion. Each religion has beautiful principles to share with others.

Instead of trying to discover the bottom line or basic principles of a religion, many people put much time and energy into questions like, "What does Buddhist philosophy say about the creation of the world?" The wise man, Shakyamuni Buddha, didn't talk about this much, but foolish guys like me talk about it. Shakyamuni Buddha kept golden silence. He said such things as,

"By the way, are you enjoying the beautiful Spring?" Later some of his disciples advised him: "We understand how you are trying to guide us through your golden silence, but most of the people misunderstand you and they think you don't know about the creation of the world. Would you show us a way to help people understand?"

So Shakyamuni Buddha told a story:

There was once a traveler going through the forest. This traveler was shot with a poisoned arrow. One of his friends who was with him said, "I want to know who the man was who shot this arrow that hit my friend. I want to know if he was a Brahmin or from the Sudra caste. I want to know if he had a dark or light complexion. I want to know why he shot the arrow, what kind of bow he used and what kind of poison he used. "

The man who was hit with the arrow had little time until the moment of this death. He said, " I only have a little time left to experience, enjoy and to appreciate life. I have only a little time to seek the meaning of life." This dying man was guiding himself into spiritual awareness.

Then Shakymuni Buddha walked away in silence.

Buddhist ministers, like Shakyamuni Buddha, have a tendency to walk away from arguments. I feel like walking away sometimes. The Buddha Dharma is teaching me and you, trying to share itself and its wisdom, so that we may guide ourselves into spiritual awareness. Shakyamuni Buddha did not argue about who is the creator of the universe. If you are thirty years old and you are able to live up to 100, you have seventy years to go. If you are fifty and able to live to eighty, you have thirty years to go. You could spend this time looking for who made this world, who made this tree, who made it snow. Or you could enjoy the tree, the snow, the world you live in. You have the freedom to go in either direction.

The Buddhist way of thinking is based on cause, condition and effect. If you get a headache, the doctor won't chop off your head. He'll examine you and try to find the cause of the headache. When he finds the cause, he's able to work to cure it. That is the cause, the condition and the effect. Buddha did the same thing. He was like a medical doctor, examining the cause of suffering. That's known as the Law of Causality, the Law of Nature.

The world is made by causes and conditions. Actually it is not made, but the world is *being* made, that is, the world is still being built. Cause and conditions so move. The world is still in the process of creation based on the laws of cause, condition and effect. You don't think about only one cause creating the whole world. "Reverend Ogui created the City of Cleveland." No. Hundreds of millions of people are creating the city of Cleveland. So it couldn't be the power of the Almighty Buddha who created the whole universe.

So how can we handle earnest questioners who ask such questions as, "Who created the world?" Here is how I handled such a situation once.

One extremely hot summer I was watering the lawn. A young lady approached me from a van. She was holding a note pad and she asked me "Are you the Reverend?"

"Yes," I replied.

Then she said she was surveying clergymen, asking them what they think about creation versus evolution.

She asked me, "What do you think about creation and evolution?"

I said, "I'm watering the lawn because it's dying."

She said, "I know! Answer my question!" She was a little frustrated.

I told her, "You don't understand that I am answering your question."

She said, "What do you mean?"

I said, "The lawn is dying, so I'm giving it water; that's the only thing I can do at this moment. Who cares about creation and evolution? I don't have such time to spend. I'm watering the lawn because it is dying." The impact inside of me was *So What?!*

I asked her how old she was and she told me her age. I told her, "You haven't much time left! You are dying! Actually, it's not a matter of age, even if you're twenty-five or thirty years old. You may die by accident or heart disease or all kinds of causes. You're talking about creation and evolution. To me such talk is a waste of time. Much more important is how you are taking care of your life here and now. I can at least give water to this lawn, which is dying."

Actually I wasn't that harsh with her. I merely told her that my watering the lawn was my answer, so write it down. She said, "No, I can't write that down."

I said, "Write it down! My answer is 'I am watering the lawn because the lawn is dying.' That's a perfect answer." She didn't write it down.

In some states people are so concerned about the creation versus evolution issue that they take cases to court to determine whether school children should be taught about creation or evolution. People on both sides of the issue are missing the point. The question again is, "What is the bottom line?" God created the earth. Fine. What is the bottom line? Learn to appreciate and to feel a little more responsible about taking care of your life and the nature around you, which are created by God. That's the point.   But people on both sides of the creation/evolution issue emphasize the theory of creation or evolution. So my answer to the lady is "That's all right." That *is* the point. If you say *That's all right,* then you are living on the right track of religious awareness.

If someone says to you,"You're going to hell because you're going to a Buddhist Temple," you can say, "That's all right." Then you've got the point of spiritual awareness. You should do the same thing if someone says you're going to heaven because you're going to a Buddhist Temple. This indicates you're free from a serious attachment to conceptualized ideas. You are living in the essence of religion. When we go to the basic principle of religion, things become very simple and we don't miss the point. The point is to realize the joy of life and feel some responsibility toward your life and all your surroundings.

What can you do with your limited life you have left? Are you going to use the limited time you have left looking for the person who shot you by a poisoned arrow or what material the arrow was made from? Or will you find joy and meaning of life in a sense of gratitude? We each have freedom of how to use our time.

I have talked too long!
From someone in the congregation, "That's all right!"

I had a chance to conduct a service in a nursing home with people who have grown old. Most of the people in this nursing home cannot stay awake even five or ten minutes. So I thought to myself, "What can I do?" I thought about Buddhist philosophy, but decided I couldn't talk about it. Well, I chanted as I did this morning, but not as long. I chanted only one verse, and then I sounded the bell. Next I said, "I am sorry and thank you." And I asked them to repeat these words four times together. You might try saying this to yourself.

UNCONDITIONAL LOVE

When I returned from my trip to Japan, I turned on my answering machine and heard four calls from the same person. The message was, "Jesus is the only savior. Believe in him and you'll be saved. Love him and you'll be loved. Anyone who does not believe in him will not be saved and will go to hell."

I think the kind of love the person who left a message on my answering machine was talking about was a very conditional love. Don't you think?

I don't know why, but then I recalled meeting with my mother in Japan. I hadn't seen her for five years. As soon as I opened the door to the house where I was born, she was standing in front of me. She held my hand and with tears in her eyes she said, "You came home."

Isn't it nice to be welcomed without any justification, whether I believe in her or not or love her or not. In a sense, I am a "bad son" to her for I live so far away that I see her seldom and I have been divorced twice. When I saw my mother, I realized that I have always been living in her love even though I forgot about her most of the time. I was grateful.

So even an ordinary person like my mother can show a love which is almost unconditional. The reason I say my mother's love was almost unconditional is because she would not show the same love to another's son.

Once I was speaking at a Methodist Church and I said, "There is no such thing as unconditional love between human beings." A man in the congregation said, "Yes, but my dog gives me unconditional love." I asked, "How?"

He said, "When I come home late drunk, my wife is in bed, but my dog is there to greet me."

Sometimes if you are busy and the dog comes around and bothers you, you may kick the dog or at least harshly tell it to go away. But the dog still loves you. We can learn from dogs. When someone kicks us or speaks to us harshly, do we still love the person?

To me Jesus Christ was a great spiritually awakened one who talked about God's love which is unconditional love. He talked about how all sentient beings could be loved. In Jodoshinshu Buddhism, one talks about Amida Buddha's compassion and wisdom which are an unconditional power to take in all sentient beings without any condition and without discrimination. This infinite compassion and wisdom breaks us out of the darkness of ignorance into infinite light and life. It is like the warmth of the sun which takes in all sentient beings without any condition. When one realizes this unconditional love or unconditional compassion and wisdom within oneself, one cannot help oneself to experience a deep spiritual sense of confession and being sorry for times we have caused trouble to others. At the same time, we feel a thankfulness and joyfulness of life. At such moments one experiences oneness with myself and non-myself. There, one's life is saved. It is nice to know we have been living in such unconditional love, unconditional compassion and wisdom of the universe whether we realize it or not, whether we care or not.

I understand that such unconditional love, universal love, does not allow any sentient being to go to hell, if there is such a place. I also understand that we have more friends in hell, if there is such a place. If we go to hell, we will keep busy shaking hands with acquaintances. You laugh. This is important. At the moment you laugh or smile, you are already in a real sense in heaven which is freed from a conceptualized hell and heaven.

An interview
with Sensei Ogui

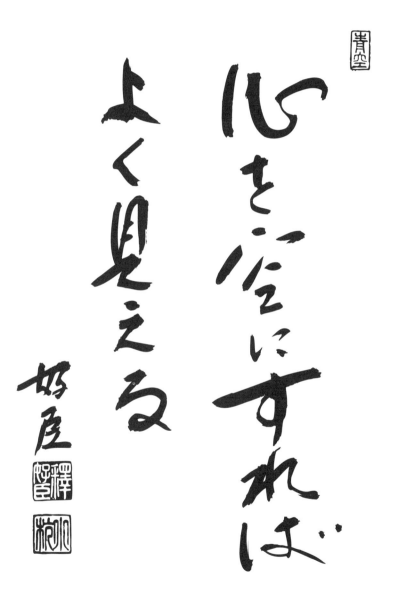

心を空にすれば
よく見える

" Freed mind, empty mind,
see things well"

*I used to think our karmic paths were
set. But now I see that they are not.
There are extremes at each end. Some
people have very little awareness and
such people seem to have little
possibility of growing. Such people
become more and more restricted and
narrow as they continually think such
thoughts as* He is so mean to me *and*
Why did this happen to me? *As
emotional beings, we cling to the past
and have curiosity as to what the future
may hold. But I can see that people
can change themselves by developing
awareness, by continually asking
themselves, "What am I aware of?
What am I learning?" By continually
asking these questions a person stays in
the here and now. In this way a person
can change the quality of cycles in his
life through awareness. He can change
the direction of his life through such
awareness.*

AN INTERVIEW WITH SENSEI OGUI

Tell us about the life of Shakyamuni Buddha.

Shakyamuni Buddha was born in India in the sixth Century
BCE. He was the son of the king of Shakya clan and was to be
the successor to his father's throne. His father kept him in the
castle and on the castle grounds *in the spring of the year*, so to
speak. He had never seen an old person, a sick person or a dead
person. I think he was an extremely sensitive boy who had lots

of questions, questions like many of us have, but I think he was more sensitive. When he went away from the castle grounds he saw an old man on the road. He asked *Why do people get old? Will I get old?* He also saw a sick person and he couldn't figure out what was happening to this person. He wondered *What is sickness? Will I suffer from sickness?* Finally, he saw a person who had died and was burning on a funeral pyre. It was shocking to him. He asked *Why do people die? Will I die?* He asked other questions like *Why do I have to meet with someone I do not like? Why do I have to be separated from my loved ones? Why do I fight with my physical desires, like being thirsty, hungry or a desire for sex? Why do I have such desires?* I have very much summarized the questions which arose in Shakyamuni Buddha's mind.

No one could give reasonable answers to his questions. At the same time he was much impressed by someone who was calm, walking in the streets, who had no home. These men were true seekers and he decided to become such a seeker, rather than becoming a king. So at the age of twenty-nine, he left his home and decided to seek the answers to these questions of human life. For six years he did all kinds of ascetic practices. He worked with several teachers. At that time some people believed that our physical strength is what builds up our desires, so they advocated that our desires could be eliminated through weakening our physical strength with different practices. So Shakyamuni Buddha did things like staying buried in the sand with only his head above ground. Or he would not eat for weeks. There were all kinds of practices at that time. Even today there are all kinds of spiritual practices. We need to be careful to think coolly and, if a practice makes sense, then take it into our lives, and if a practice doesn't feel comfortable to us or make sense to us, we need to learn to leave it alone.

Shakyamuni eventually realized that if he weakened his physical strength, he could not continue his seeking to find the answers to his questions. He was extremely weak and Sujata, a young woman, brought him a bowl of milk. He began gaining strength. She also washed his body. He decided to sit under a Bodhi tree until he became enlightened. At the age of thirty-five years he became enlightened and began sharing his awareness of Universal truth. He taught until his death at the age of eighty. Shakyamuni Buddha was a human being and he died as a human being. His enlightenment is the spirit of awareness, a treasure. Shakyamuni Buddha's final message at his death is as follows:

> The person who sees merely my body only is not the one who truly sees me. The person who sees the Universal Truth is the one who truly sees me. After my death, the Dharma shall be your teacher. Follow the Dharma and you will be true to me. The true Buddha is not a human body, it is enlightenment. A human body must die, but the wisdom of enlightenment will exist forever in the truth or Dharma and in the practice of Dharma.

After his death Buddhist teachings and practices evolved into two streams: Mahayana Buddhism and Theravada Buddhism. Mahayana Buddhism is taught and practiced in Tibet, Mongolia, China, Korea and Japan. Mahayana Buddhism emphasizes practices which can be done by anyone who so chooses. Theravada Buddhism is taught and practiced in Ceylon, Cambodia, Burma and Thailand. It emphasizes the precepts for the laymen and monastic practices for monks. Both streams have been brought to the United States. To me, this is truly the *United States* where the different Buddhist teachings and practices are united.

I want to know about Dharma. What is Dharma?

I became a so-called Buddhist minister thirty-two years ago and I have been working in this capacity since then. Before that, I was at a Buddhist training center similar to a monastery. I was a serious student seeking to know what is Dharma. While in this training center, I participated in a rigorous schedule. One morning I asked my teacher, "Would you share with me a taste of Dharma?"

He looked at me and said, "Did you have breakfast?"

I said, "Yes, I did." But in my mind I was thinking, "What is he talking about?" I had asked such a big question, "What is Dharma?" in contrast with the mundane response "Did you have breakfast?"

My teacher looked at me again knowing I was serious.

I was quiet.

He said further, "By the way, do you know what you ate for breakfast?"

I recalled what I had eaten and told him.

He said, "Many people don't recall what they have eaten." He continued, "You know what you ate, but you don't know what you received of the life of others."

I still didn't understand what he was talking about.

He said, "Did you appreciate the breakfast?" He smiled; I think he was reading my mind. He continued, "There is no Dharma besides your life itself."

I still couldn't understand.

Time passed. One rainy day my teacher asked me to take a letter to his friend who lived in the next village. I was proud to do this errand for my teacher. Coming back to the training center, I was soaked from rain and he was waiting for me at the door of the temple. When I stepped into the temple I felt an impact as his eyes gazed at me. He asked, "What did you realize?" I felt proud of what I had done for my teacher, I hadn't thought about *What did I realize?*

I went to my room and changed my soaking clothes. When I returned to the hallway, he asked me again, "What did you realize?" This question had quite an impact on me. It scared me in a sense. I couldn't answer. He smiled at me and said, "You got wet on this errand. When we walk in the rain, we all get wet . . . and this is Dharma." He walked away.

I was astonished. Still to this day I continue to have a vivid memory of this interaction with my teacher.

With the perspective of 32 more years of living in Dharma, I can add to this understanding. Whether you are Christian, Jewish, Muslim, Buddhist, a man or a woman, young or old, black, yellow, white, Japanese, Chinese, German or American, whatever you believe -- when we walk in the rain, we all get wet. This is Universal Truth; this is Dharma. Whereever we are, time is passing. We are each getting older. We each go through experiences of anger, happiness, joy, sadness and so on. However, whatever we are feeling, it is still true: *When we walk in the rain, we get wet.*

We each are going through the path of our lives. So often we think such things as, *I am a Christian; He is a Buddhist; I am a man; She is a woman.* Rather, the essence for each of us is that we each will get wet. We each are living in such limited time. And living means we are each dying. Buddhist scholars organize teachings logically; in their organizational scheme one part of the Law of Nature is the Law of Impermanence. This law emphasizes that things are constantly changing, becoming and moving on. Whatever condition you are in, things are moving on. Are you aware that your life is constantly changing? That you are constantly becoming? Are you aware of this true aspect of life?

It is true for each of us that things are changing and becoming. The purpose of Buddhist training is to become aware of the changing nature of our individual lives. This is a true aspect of each of our lives.   This is the Universal Truth or Dharma. This aspect of life does not depend on what a person believes or what a text says. Many people make statements like *The Bible says* . . .*The Buddhist Sutra says* . . .No, this doesn't matter. What matters is the extent you are aware of the changing nature of your being.

Green leaves are changing colors. This is a true fact. Universal Truth is Dharma. This is a logical explanation, but the impact has to come from experience.

So is a student of Dharma constantly thinking about Dharma?

I am talking with you right now. This is part of my awareness of Dharma. It's amazing, in a sense. Fantastic even. I didn't expect that I would be here in my office talking with you. Of course, we both knew about this meeting because you made an appointment to meet with me. But ten, twenty, even 100 years ago, we did not know that we would meet each other at this here and now. Our meeting is part of this manifestation of *things as they are.* This is Dharma. This is not a matter of good or bad. We may say *I had a good day* or *This is not my day.* Universal

Truth is beyond the cheap judgements of good, bad, right, wrong. Rather a person who has an awareness of the Universal Truth may think *So it is. It is amazing to be as it is.*

When a dear friend dies, it is common for us to say something like *I can't believe that he is dead. I just saw him yesterday.* Believe it. Truth manifests itself beyond our beliefs. In our culture the importance of our beliefs is emphasized. We particularly place significance on the knowledge in books. Universal Truth is not necessarily the knowledge in Buddhist texts. The truth is *he is dead* whether I believe it or not. Realizing, accepting that a dear friend is dead, is a way of realizing Dharma or Universal Truth. Most often, we petty human beings do not truly realize Dharma or *things as they are.*

So accepting is part of what you are talking about? Accepting the Universal Truth? Is that it?

I think so. In order to accept, we have to realize. First, one needs to open her eyes and see it, understand it, realize it and be aware. From there acceptance comes through. Of course, there are short cuts, that is acceptance without any examination or comprehension. Some people in religious training don't want to go through experiences to gain understanding or realization. They simply want to come into believing. If he or she is on the right track, that shortcut makes sense. But much of time, we depend on religious teachers and teachings. Sometimes, in the name of religion, teachers do things which aren't beneficial, so we need to be careful.

Would you say there is good and bad Dharma? For example, if you don't do something, is it bad? And if you do it, is it good?

From the aspect of Dharma, every event in your life is good. Sad happenings are good; happy happenings are good. For each of us, whatever happens in our lives, there is always an impact of life events. We need to ask ourselves, "What am I aware of from this impact?"

Any experience can be viewed from different perspectives. For example, you and I talking like this can be viewed from a financial perspective. A lawyer may charge seventy-five dollars for forty-five minutes of conferencing. Even though I have as extensive training and experiences as such a lawyer, I have no charge for this interview with you. So from the financial perspective, this interview is bad for me and good for you. Thus, such judgements of good and bad, for example that this interview is "bad" for me, are very uncertain. But this interview is an aspect of Dharma. It is such a great meeting with someone who sincerely asks questions. It's fantastic! Concerning judgments related to spirituality or awareness of Dharma, every event is great, absolutely good. The best of life is to be aware of the truth.

When I visit a prisoner, I ask *What are you aware of? What do you realize?* We all think killing and stealing are ethically and morally wrong. We all hate to have painful experiences. But instead of viewing each experience as good or bad, a person who is advancing herself spiritually asks herself *What am I aware of?* In this way, the person views life beyond her judgements of good and bad. Rather she sees the absolute good in each experience. You may lose your friend or your mother or father. You may be in the midst of a divorce case. You may view these situations as sad or bad or unfortunate. But from a spiritual point of view, from an advanced stage of awareness of Dharma -- It's great! So the key point in such experiences is *What do you learn from the experience?*

How does Dharma relate to Karma?

Karma is like a stream of water. Karma is each one's path of life. Often one asks *Why me?* The answer is *Because of you.* Karma is your path to go through. We continually make moral and ethical judgements of our karmic life events by saying to ourselves such phrases as *This is good. This is bad. This is right. This is wrong.* But when we have an awareness of Dharma, our karmic path experiences are not a matter of good, bad, right or wrong. Rather we think *So it is.* This is our path to go through.

In sum, each of us has a unique karmic path to go through. An important part of enriching our lives concerns our awareness of Dharma or Universal Truth. Through such awareness one can change the quality of one's life. You may ask *How can this be done?* Again I say, in each experience in your karmic stream, ask yourself *What am I aware of?*

Ten people may listen to what I say. Each of these ten people will take what I say in different ways. Each listener has a different quality of their receiver like the earphone component of a Walkman. *What is the quality of each of these earphones? What do they receive? How much do they receive? This is a key point.*

Take the example of a man who has contracted AIDS. Such a man cannot ignore what is happening to his body and is likely to feel much anger and depression. Many people come through difficulties in their lives and at death they don't know what they lived for. This may be true for one man dying of AIDS and not for another such man. Each of these men, each of us as well, have opportunities to be aware. So guide yourself to be aware of Dharma.

You actually don't need a teacher because the experiences you have in your life are great teachers. We each live in a world of master teachers. Our daily experiences are our masters. To me anger is great, depression is great, happiness is great, charity is great. *What do we think about? Do our actions take advantage of others? Are we creating regrets or feelings of shame for ourselves and others? What do we do for others?* Continually ask yourself such questions. Then you will see how Dharma relates to karma in your life.

What is the difference between someone who does not realize and accept Dharma as much as someone who does?

I've been working for thirty-two years with temple members. I observe their actions. Some financially support the temple. Some give their time and energy. Some come to services only to keep up friendships with others in the Sangha, a gathering of people seeking the Dharma. Others come to hear so-called Buddhist teaching and put effort in living what they learn. So I observe huge differences in people's actions toward the temple and toward Buddhist training and teaching.

What do I do for those people who don't realize it? I can hope and I keep sharing. I smile at my karmic path. I frequently think to myself *Why am I doing this every Sunday for years and years?* I repeat the same teachings over and over again. I know what I can do may be small. Yet, I keep sharing. Some day, some time, someone may have some kind of impact from my sharing. The Buddhist way is not to preach. Buddhists do not try to convert people. If Buddhism makes sense to people, they will come to the temple to learn Buddhist practices and teachings.

I think Buddhism is a very beneficial movement in today's society. *There are 84,000 paths to go through. There is not one path.* Buddhism traveled from India to Tibet and to China to Korea and then to Japan. Now it is coming to America. The domestic religion of Japan is Shinto in which practitioners worship 84,000 Gods. So when missionaries brought Christianity into Japan, Japanese were not bothered by One God coming into Japan. The Oriental religions like Shinto, Buddhism, Confucianism do not emphasize having The God, One God, The Right God. Thus, there is little history of bloodshed around religions in Japan.

As a trustee of the World Parliament of Religion, I have observed some religious leaders who cannot sit together. To me this is amazing, ridiculous. People get hung up on the question *What do you believe?* When people ask me this, sometimes I compromise and say *I believe in Universal Truth.* Others talk about *What do you believe about Jesus Christ?* I say that what you learn from Jesus Christ is much more important. I think Jesus Christ was a great master teacher. He shared compassion, love and wisdom. He was aware of the Universal Truth, so learn from his teachings, his actions, from his life.

At times Muslims and Christians have difficulties spending time together. It's sad when people miss the essence of their religions.

Would you say that if a person realizes and accepts the Universal Truth or Dharma to a great extent, then this would be the best for this person's karmic cycle?

I don't know what is best. But at least I could see enrichment and meaning in such a person's life. Such a person would always be learning, endlessly being aware. Such a person is very comfortable to be with; such a person is very much needed in this world; such a person has a feeling of freedom. Dharma does not limit a person. The life of such a person is the manifestation of Dharma. Such a person lives in a way that benefits her own life and the lives of others.

How does Dharma relate to the Four Noble Truths and the Eightfold Path?

Dharma itself has no form, no color. It always manifests into life as form and as color. Green leaves are changing colors, showing us the law of impermanence, showing us that things are changing and becoming.

The Four Noble Truths with the Eightfold Path is an organized, systematized way of guiding people into the awareness of Dharma. The first noble truth is that in life, that is birth, old age and death, there is suffering. The second noble truth is that the cause of suffering is being attached to life. We create suffering because we have a self-centered, egoistic view. Further, we create difficulties through ignorance because we can't see things as they are. Most of the time we see what we want to see. This is the third noble truth. The fourth noble truth is that there is a path away from this suffering. The path is the Eightfold Path, consisting of right view, right thoughts, right speech, right action, right effort, right livelihood, right wisdom, and right meditation. These are easy to talk about, but hard to practice. Someone has to talk about it, so I am!

The Four Noble Truths and the Eightfold Path are life steps. The first of the Eightfold Path is the most important. It has to do with not viewing the world in terms of right and wrong, but to view things in our lives in an absolute sense and to see things as they are. When we can do this, the other parts of the Eightfold Path fall into place.

So the Four Noble Truths with the Eightfold Path is a systematized way, similar to a textbook, which can help people who are not aware of Dharma. They are like a bridge to cross over. Actually people do not need such steps to enjoy life *as it is*. It is like falling in love. Two people falling in love do not argue or even talk about *What is love?* Rather they go through the experience and are aware of what is happening in their lives. Or take a husband and wife who have lived together for fifty years. They know what love is, but they can't describe it or how it came about. It just happens.

So the Four Noble Truths and the Eightfold Path are organized, systematized way to cross into Dharma. We need to practice having the Right View, the Absolute View. We need to practice meditation. As we meditate, if we can drop our preconceived ideas for even ten seconds, then instead of naming the trees, we can relax and see the tree. At such times Dharma will talk to us.

So we are living in the Dharma. We human beings are like a person swimming in Lake Superior thirstily calling, "Give me water." But unless the time comes, we do not truly get the impact and realize we are surrounded with water. The time needs to be right. For example, your mother may say something to you when you are eight years old. You hear it and you think you understand it. Then when you are thirty and you have a child of your own, you remember what your mother said and you truly understand it. The time was right.

I am not talking about intellectual understanding. When people in Buddhist training begin talking about what they believe or what they have learned intellectually, teachers will cut it off. Understanding Dharma is more than intellectual understanding. So whatever I say -- at the right time -- Bang -- it has an impact. So teachers and masters must work with patience and understanding, often waiting for persons to understand.

What about the Buddhist Precepts? How do they relate to spiritual growth?

There are five Buddhist Precepts for lay persons to follow. These precepts relate to how people live their lives. Some people need the Precepts to encourage them to practice the Buddha Dharma. The five Precepts are *Try not to take others' lives; Try not to take what is not given; Try not to be involved in hurtful sexual relations; Try not to lie; Try not to drink intoxicants.* People who are proud that they observe all of these precepts are still beginners of Buddha Dharma and beginners in practicing the Buddha Dharma.

The precepts are basic practices for anyone who follows the Buddhist path. *When you realize that you cannot keep even one of these, then you are stepping into deeper spirituality.* For example, when you take even one step, you kill hundreds of invisible beings. Even when vegetarians eat, a living plant has been killed for their diet. Another example has to do with intoxicants. You may drink an intoxicant to warm yourself and enjoy it. However, it is a different situation if you get drunk and begin fighting and damage things around you. Extensive drinking can also damage the organs in your body. Your body can tell you, "Hey! Hey! Stop drinking so much." If you listen to your body, it will tell you when to stop drinking. Sometimes people concentrate on how others do not follow the precepts. Rather, reflect on these precepts and how they relate to your own spirituality through deeper spirituality.

Does meditation practice help someone realize Dharma?

Meditation helps me calm myself and harmonize myself. Once we harmonize our bodies and minds, we can settle down and drop all preconceived notions.   Then we can see the manifestation of Dharma as it is.

Is each person's Karmic path predestined?   Or can a person change her path?

I used to think our karmic paths were set. But now I see that they are not. There are extremes at each end. Some people have very little awareness and such people seem to have little possibility of growing. Such people become more and more restricted and narrow as they continually think such thoughts as *He is so mean to me* and *Why did this happen to me?* But I can see that people can change themselves by developing awareness, by continually asking themselves *What am I aware of? What am I learning?* Through this way of living, the quality of life can be changed. By continually asking these questions, a person stays in the here and now, which is much emphasized in Buddhism. Buddhists do not talk much about the past and the future, before and after. The past and the future do not make sense without awareness of how I am *right now.* Buddhism does not emphasize before life or after life. What is important is *this life, this moment.* What is the impact of you and me talking here and now? This is *real*. Tomorrow your heart or my heart may stop. You or I may be hit by a car. Here and now is the absolute moment, the eternal now. This moment cannot be repeated again. As emotional beings, we cling to the past and have curiosity of what the future may hold. When one focuses on what I am doing right now, there is a continuation of eternity.

Even a person with terminal cancer will benefit from this way of living. With this moment by moment proceeding through our lives, we will take actions based on our acceptance and realization of the way things are. The quality of energy in our karmic path is thus changed.

I do have a consciousness of creating a better karmic path. But I know this consciousness, as well as my judgements of good and bad, is uncertain. I observe others. I notice a person stealing a purse at a store, another person comes and truly listens to the teachings. I know in the absolute sense each of these actions is not good or bad. *They just are.*

Often I have a consciousness of actions which are *good* or *bad,* yet I know this is not real. When I do not have such a consciousness of *good* and *bad* actions, then maybe I truly am doing *good.* I smile at myself a lot.

Here we are talking together. My inner spirit arises as we exchange conversation like this, because I feel your sincerity. If you were not sincere, I would excuse myself.

Here is another example of this idea of changing the quality of our lives, changing our karmic paths. People were disappointed when Michael Jordan announced his retirement from basketball. He said, "I have to go one step forward." Similarly there is a story often told to people in Buddhist training. A man climbed up a tree, putting much effort into getting to the top of the tree. The teacher's response was *Go one step further.* The man retorted, "If I go one step further, I will fall down and die." The teacher still says *Go one step further.* Only a very dedicated person will take up this challenge. Buddhist wisdom says *Keep walking through it.* Don't get stuck there.

What about beliefs? How do they contribute to changing the quality of our lives?

We each have to go through life experiences according to our karmic path. Think about this rather than thinking such thoughts as *If I believe this, then I am saved. If I believe that, I am a good person and God will take care of me.* Many religious people, and I am talking about people of any religion -- Buddhism, Christianity, Judaism, whatever -- emphasize beliefs and thus encourage people to think in this way. To me, any religion is like the finger pointing to the beauty of the moon. The religion and its beliefs are not the beauty of the moon itself. The beauty of the moon just is. It needs no title. Each religion has a name for the actual beauty of the moon, the embodiment of wisdom, love and compassion. Buddhists call it Buddha. Christians call it God. Muslims call it Allah. Each of these are only names. Actually a title is not needed. In the absolute sense it might be called *no title, no name.* But we need names in order to conveniently communicate. In the real sense of life itself, we don't need such a name.

Many religious people are stuck on the finger or the beliefs of their religion. They think that these beliefs are the beauty of the moon. When people say such phrases as *The Bible says . . .* or *The Buddhist text says . . .* or refer to the Ten Commandments or the Buddhist Precepts, they are stuck on the finger pointing to the moon or the format. When I am with people who are stuck on the format, I do not feel comfortable. When such people talk about their beliefs and theories, they end up arguing, even fighting. When a person is hung up on such concepts, a master teacher will say *Go through it.*

How does one on a spiritual path get past the finger and actually become aware of or experience the beauty of the moon?

Each experience is a gift, even a so-called *bad* experience. *What is important is an individual's nature to learn from any experience.* Secondly, we need friends with wisdom and compassion who can share insights with us. You may have at least one friend who will say *Hey, wait a minute,* and then show us a different point of view. We'd rather talk only with friends who agree with us and go along with what we say. But we don't learn too much in this case. So have one friend who has wisdom and will not always agree with you.

How do you know if you are on the right track? A person who thinks he is always right is probably not on the right track. Such a person emphasizes his or her beliefs and does not listen to others. Such a person does not learn much, does not change or expand his or her thinking. His thinking can be squeezed into a small shell.

In contrast, there is a person who has reached the point of realizing the beauty of the moon. It does not matter with which religion others identify this person. Such a person shares this realization with others. When you are with such a person, you feel comfortable. Such a person naturally shares love, compassion and wisdom. You may have a cup of coffee with such a person and without saying anything, enjoy sharing the time together.

So how do you work with your own nature? How do you get past focusing on the finger and experience the beauty of the moon? So whatever religion you are, please do not get stuck focusing on the finger.

Short concluding
Dharma talks

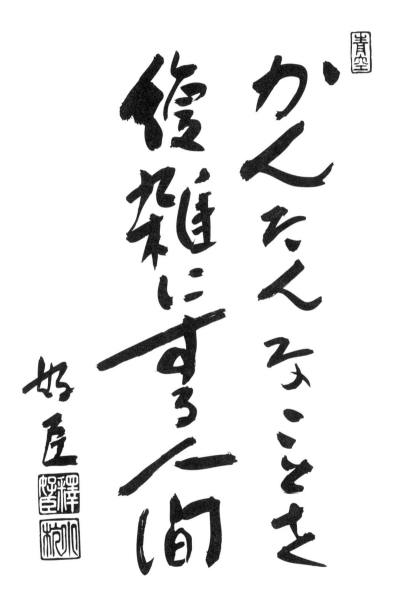

" We humans make a
simple thing complicated"

I APPRECIATE SMALL KINDNESSES

This morning as I talked with a scratchy throat, Naomi brought me a glass of water to the podium. I appreciate such small kindnesses.

Earlier this morning as I was having breakfast at the Holiday Inn, a couple slowly walked in. They each had wrinkles on their faces from aging. Actually they could hardly walk. I think they were having breakfast before going to church. The man pulled the chair out from under the table for the woman. I smiled . . . . What a beautiful scene. Small kindnesses are very attractive.

CHOOSE ONE SMALL PRACTICE

People struggle to build up spiritual securities and happiness. They put energy into learning from the different religious traditions. Sometimes people attend workshops and seminars. They spend time and money in this way. They keep attending and learning. Actually they don't have to keep doing this.

Instead, choose one small practice and keep reflecting on it and doing it. Then you will understand everything. For example, in Christianity you are told, "Love your neighbor." Sincerely practice this and observe yourself as you practice. You may smile at yourself when you see how difficult it is. From there a spiritual gate will open up to you.

PEACE IN THIS WORLD?

One morning I took a taxi to one of the sessions of the Council of the Parliament of World Religions. I was wearing priestly clothes. The taxi driver asked me, "Are you going to the Parliament of Religions?"

I said, "Yes."

He said, "Do you think peace will come to this world?"

I said, "I don't know."

I could tell he was happy to hear my answer. Then he perceptively asked me, "What are you doing then? You are wasting your time, man."

I said, "At least I'm paying you for driving me in your taxi, you know."

He looked back at me and we laughed. I said, "Hey, wait a minute. At this moment you and I are laughing together. This is the first step of peace between us."

He said, "You are an interesting guy."

We laughed again.

This taxi driver and I shared a piece of peace without much consciousness, without effort.

ARE YOU WEALTHY?

A wealthy man who lived in Cleveland looked up into the sky on a cloudy, rainy day and wished for a blue sky. He decided to go to California to buy a blue sky so he could always have one. When he got to California, sure enough there was a blue sky there, but no one would sell a piece of it to him. The man knew that Hawaii is known for its blue sky, so he went to Hawaii to buy a blue sky. In Hawaii, as in California, he basked in the sun under a blue sky but no one would sell him some blue sky. He then went to India, a country known world-wide for its spirituality, but even there no one would sell him even a small piece of blue sky. Finally, exhausted, he returned to Cleveland. He woke up the next morning. As he drank some coffee he looked out of the kitchen window. Into his consciousness came the sound of birds chirping, then some branches on a cherry tree in his yard and, behind the tree branches, he became aware of *blue sky*. He realized that infinite love and compassion were all around him. He realized that he had been living in the *blue sky*.

JUST GO AWAY

Once, when I was in San Francisco watching TV at my apartment, someone knocked on the door. I wasn't expecting anyone. I opened the door and Susuki Roshi was standing right there. Susuki Roshi is the author of *Zen Mind, Beginner's Mind* and the founder of the San Francisco Zen Center. I was surprised to see him.

I said, "Come in! This is nice. Let's make some tea."

He said that people in his temple had gathered and they were talking about the future directions of the temple. They had a certain kind of vibration as they talked. He listened to them for a while, and then he disappeared; he ran away.

That's interesting, isn't it? Sometimes Buddhist monks and masters and other spiritual people just disappear. They do like that.

Sometimes, but not all the time, what a spiritual seeker can do is just be quiet . . . or just run away from people who cannot get along. When people around you have a certain vibration and you feel like, "Geez, it's hard to be in here," you can make an excuse to go to the rest room and just go away.

TREES

There is no doubt the leaves on the trees are changing color, showing the law of impermanence. Things are changing and becoming.

If I were a tree, I would say, "I want to keep all these leaves. They are so beautiful! People admire me because my leaves are such gorgeous colors. I want to continue to hold these leaves with my pride. I don't want to let these vivid leaves go".

Suppose I get my way and the leaves remain on the branches. Winter sets in. Snow piles up on the leaves which miraculously are clinging to my branches. The weight of the snow breaks my branches. Crack! Crack!"

This is what each one of us does. We each think, "I must protect myself! I must keep this position, this recognition, this pride -- whatever!" At the end of the day we each one think, "I am so exhausted!" Yet, we don't want to let go.

Real trees are amazing! Before winter sets in, they do not cling to their golden leaves, they lose their leaves, they become open, naked in a sense. They accept what comes.

Heart Sutra

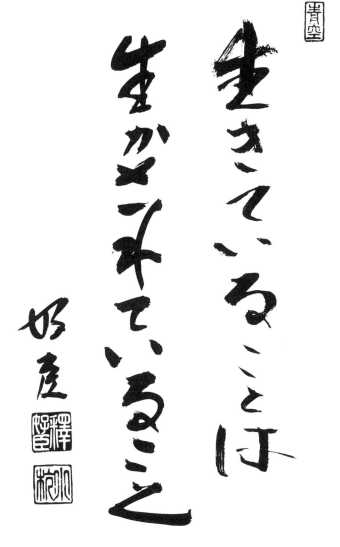

生きていることは
生かされていること

"To live is to be lived."

The Heart Sutra

Avalokitesvara, Bodhisattva of Compassion, observing deeply the Perfection of Wisdom, Prajna Paramita, clearly saw the emptiness of the Five Aggregates, thus transcending adversity and pain.   O Sariputra, Form is no other than Emptiness, Emptiness no other than Form, Form is exactly Emptiness, Emptiness exactly Form, the same is true of Feeling, Perception, Mental formations and Consciousness.   O Sariputra, all dhramas are forms of Emptiness, not born, not destroyed; not tainted, not pure; not increasing, not decreasing. And so in Emptiness there is no Form, no Feeling, no Perception, no Mental Formations, no Consciousness; no eyes, no ears, no nose, no tongue, no body, no mind; no color, no smell, no taste, no touch, no thought; no realm of sight and so forth until no realm of consciousness; no ignorance, no end to ignorance and so forth until no old age and death and no end to old age and death; no suffering, no desire, no cessation, no path, no wisdom, no attainment.   And so the Bodhisattva relies on the Prajna Paramita with no hindrance in the mind, no hindrance, therefore no fear; far beyond deluded thoughts, this is Nirvana.   All past, present and future Buddhas rely on the Perfection of Wisdom and thus attain the Highest Perfect Enlightenment.   Therefore, know that the Prajna Paramita is the Great Transcendent Mantra, the Great Resplendent Mantra, the Unexcelled Mantra, the Unsurpassed Mantra, the Mantra which Relieves All Suffering, so proclaim the Prajna Paramita Mantra, proclaim the Mantra and say: *Gate! Gate! Parasamgate! Bodhi, Satha!* Clear Perfection of Wisdom, Prajna Paramita Heart Sutra.

Glossary

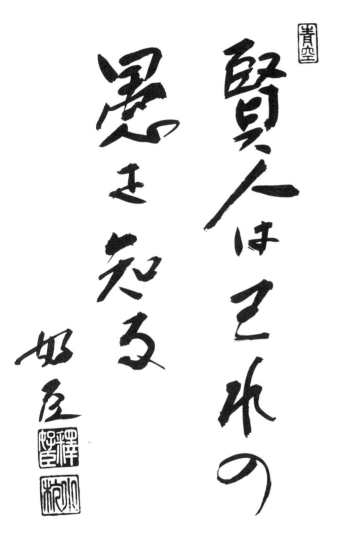

" A wise person knows his own foolishness "

GLOSSARY

Amida Buddha -- infinite light and infinite life, light stands for wisdom and life stands for compassion; a dynamic spiritual power that one awakens to a truth of life which lies beyond our normal, self-centered thinking and guides us into a joy of spiritual life.

bodhisattva -- one who makes vows to attain one's own enlightenment and at the same time to work toward others' enlightennment.

Buddha -- three meanings: 1) the historical Buddha, a man in India named Shakyamuni Buddha who was enlightened to the Dharma, the universal truth, over 2500 years ago; 2) Buddha Nature which is a part of every being, our nature to realize we are enlightened; 3) a symbol of power of infinite light and life, wisdom and compassion called Amida Buddha.

Buddha Dharma -- Buddhism, the Universal Truth that a Buddha realizes.

Buddha Nature -- the seed of enlightenment in every being, our potential to become fully awake or enlightened.

dana -- the practice of giving and receiving; charity which is one of six practices for spiritual advancement.

Dharma -- a universal truth which is beyond our beliefs, *Dharma* manifests in our life as things as they are.

Dhammapada (in pali) or *Dharmaa pada* (in Sanskrit) -- a collection of verses comprising the basic teaching of what the historical Buddha, Shakyamuni Buddha, taught.

Dokusan -- a private interview with a master or spiritual teacher in which one testifies one's realization.

dukkha -- mental functions which disturb and pollute the mind and body; impurity, depravity, affliction, evil passion, defilement.

enlightenment -- an ultimate reality, universal truth which becomes one's life   through awareness and realization.

Issei – first generation Japanese American

gassho -- placing palms together, a way of humbleness, thankfulness, and mindfulness.

hakujin -- white race.

Jodoshinshu -- a Pure Land sect of Buddhism (see Shin also).

koan -- a question which breaks through the intellectual thinking, and opens up a simple and direct way of awareness.

Mahayana -- the "great vehicle" which means all beings; all people with any situation are able to practice this school of Buddhist tradition and it's teaching.

Namu Amida Butsu -- *Namu* (in Sanskrit) means 'I take refuge in' or 'I put myself in.' *Amida Butsu* is a cause of the cosmos which manifests into our world as an 'infinite light' (Amitabha) and infinite life (Amitayus). The infinite light manifests into our life as a means of infinite wisdom and the infinite life as infinite compassion. Hence, *Namu Amida Butsu* means 'I put myself in infinite wisdom and compassion' to realize that 'I am living in the light of infinite wisdom and compassion.' For Nembutsu (Namu Amida Butsu) followers, this is a life-time realization on what this means in their lives.

Na man da bu – a shortened form of Namu Amida Butsu

Nembutsu – See Namu Amida Butsu

Nisei -- second generation Japanese American .

Obon -- a traditional Japanese celebration welcoming, honoring and joining all the beings who came before us including our ancestors. Obon is celebrated in July or August with lanterns and dancing. It is a time to realize one's life exists with a connection to others' lives.

practice -- ways of cultivating the mind and the heart, e.g. Zen meditation and walking meditation are practices. Practices are set according to each school or sect of Buddhist traditions. In a wider sense, a *practice* is seeing each experience as a gift not to be ignored. What we learn from the experience is what we get and what we are and what we will be.

prajna -- transcendental wisdom. The wisdom of the enlightened one, the Buddha.

prajna paramita -- wisdom practice to guide us to perfection; the six stages of spiritual perfection are the practice of charity, morality, patience, vigor, meditation, and wisdom.

precepts -- aspirations or vows to discipline oneself to follow a right path or Buddhist practice. Precepts common for lay people are *Do not take an others' life. Do not steal. Do not indulge in hurtful sexuality. Do not lie or gossip. Do not become intoxicated by drink or drugs.*

sangha -- a group of people who practice together and seek the Dharma, the Universal Truth

sesshin -- a scheduled time for participants' minds and hearts to get in touch with a true reality through the practices of walking, sitting, chanting, and listening meditations.

Shin -- a shortened form of Jodoshinshu sect, a school of Mahayana Buddhism which was begun by Shinran (1173 - 1263) in Japan

Shakaymuni Buddha – The historical Buddha born in India 2500 years ago; he guided himself into enlightenment through awareness of Dharma.

Shinran -- A man who brought Buddhism from monastic life to the life of ordinary people. He openly married. He asked the question, "What Buddhist teachings can be practiced with a wife and children?" He could not compromise his endless passions and desires and with this desperation he realized that he could abandon himself into infinite compassion and wisdom.

skandhas -- the five causally-conditioned elements of existence which form a being or entity. The five constituent elements forming a human body are 1) matter or form, 2) perception, 3) conception, 4) volition, and 5) consciousness. They form a human being in temporal or phenomenal nature so that non-isolated self or ego can understand what happens under the law of impermanence.

Sunyata (Sanskrit) -- often translated as 'voidness' or 'emptiness'; Sunyata does not deny the concept of existence as such, but hold that all existence and the constituent elements which make up existence are dependent upon causation. "Sunyata is no other than form and form is no other that Sunyata.", are words of wisdom concerning freeing ourselves from   attachments and seeing things are they truly are.

sutra (Sanskit) -- scriptures which convey the teaching of Shakyamuni Buddha

Theravada -- the way of the elders. The Theravada School covers Ceylon, Burma, Siam, and Cambodia which is called the Southern School; Theravada used to be identified as Hinnayana School, in contrast to the Northern or Mahayana School which covers Tibet, Mongolia, China, Korea, and Japan.

Zazen (Japanese) -- sitting meditation to let one's self become free from attachments and explore the harmony of body and mind. Zazen is part of Zen training.

Zen -- (Japanese; Dhyana in Sanskrit, Ch'an in Chinese) generally translated as meditation. Zen is the act of discovering oneself;   Zen is described as a special transmission (or enlightenment) outside the scriptures; no dependence on words and letters; direct pointing to the nature of man; seeing into one's nature, and the attainment of Buddhahood. Zen sometimes means a Zen School of Buddhism.

How to Order
Zen Shin Talks by Sensei Ogui
Price: $14.95

Call toll free 1-800- 247-6553

e-mail: order@ bookmaster.com
fax: 419 281-6883
mailing address: BookMasters, Inc.
                          P.O. Box 388
                          Ashland, OH 44805

Available after October 2, 1998

For more information about *Zen Shin Buddhist Publications*:

Call 1- 216- 321-4938

e-mail: marygove1@juno.com
fax: 216 321-4978